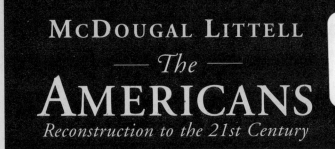

M

In-Depth Resources: Unit 7

Passage to a New Century

A HOUGHTON MIFFLIN COMPANY

Evanston, Illinois • Boston • Dallas

Acknowledgments

CHAPTER 24

Excerpt from *All the President's Men* by Carl Bernstein and Bob Woodward. Copyright © 1974 by Carl Bernstein and Bob Woodward. Reprinted with the permission of Simon & Schuster.

Excerpt from *Love Canal: My Story* by Lois Marie Gibbs with Murray Levine. Copyright © 1982 by Lois Gibbs and Murray Levine. Reprinted by permission of Lois Marie Gibbs.

Excerpt from *Silent Spring* by Rachel Carson. Copyright © 1962 by Rachel L. Carson. Copyright © renewed 1990 by Roger Christie. Reprinted by permission of Houghton Mifflin Company. All rights reserved.

Excerpt from *Memories of the Ford Administration* by John Updike. Copyright © 1992 by John Updike. Reprinted by permission of Alfred A. Knopf, Inc.

CHAPTER 25

Excerpt from *The Great Divide* by Studs Terkel. Copyright © 1988 by Studs Terkel. Reprinted by permission of Pantheon Books, a division of Random House, Inc.

Excerpt from *It Doesn't Take a Hero* by General H. Norman Schwarzkopf and Peter Petre. Copyright © 1992 by H. Norman Schwarzkopf. Reprinted by permission of Bantam Books, a division of Bantam Doubleday Dell Publishing Group, Inc.

Excerpt from *The Bonfire of the Vanities* by Tom Wolfe. Copyright © 1987 by Tom Wolfe. Reprinted by permission of Farrar, Straus & Giroux, Inc.

"Salvador Late or Early," from *Woman Hollering Creek and Other Stories* by Sandra Cisneros. Copyright © 1991 by Sandra Cisneros. Published by Vintage Books, a division of Random House, Inc., New York. Reprinted by permission of Susan Bergholz Literary Services, New York.

CHAPTER 26

Excerpt from *The Road Ahead* by Bill Gates. Copyright © 1995 by William H. Gates III. Used by permission of Viking Penguin, a division of Penguin Books USA Inc.

"Immigrants" by Pat Mora is reprinted with permission from the publisher of *Borders* (Houston: Arte Público Press, University of Houston, 1986).

"Latin Women Pray," from *Reaching for the Mainland and Selected New Poems* by Judith Ortiz Cofer. Copyright © 1995 by Bilingual Press/Editorial Bilingüe. Reprinted by permission of Bilingual Press/Editorial Bilingüe, Arizona State University, Tempe, AZ.

"Mexicans Begin Jogging" by Gary Soto, first published in *The Americas Review*, Volume 9, No. 1, 1981. Reprinted by permission of Chronicle Books.

"Modern Secrets," from *Monsoon History* by Shirley Geok-lin Lim (London: Skoob, 1995). Reprinted by permission of the author.

"Saying Yes" by Diana Chang, first published in *Asian-American Heritage: An Anthology of Prose and Poetry*, edited by David Hsin-Fu Wand. Copyright © 1974 by Diana Chang. Reprinted by permission of the author.

Printed in the United States of America.

ISBN-13: 978-0-618-17612-0   ISBN-10: 0-618-17612-8

9 10 11 12 – MDO – 08 07 06

CHAPTER 26 The United States in Today's World, 1992–2001

Name _____ Date _____

GUIDED READING *The Nixon Administration*

A. As you read about the Nixon administration, take notes to describe President
Nixon's policies toward the problems facing him.

Problems	Policies
1. Size and power of the federal government	
2. Inefficiency of the welfare system	
3. Vietnam War and domestic disorder	
4. Nixon's reelection	
5. Liberalism of Supreme Court justices	
6. Stagflation and recession	
7. U.S.–China relations	
8. U.S.–Soviet relations	

B. On the back of this paper, explain the significance of **realpolitik** and **OPEC**
during the Nixon years.

Name _____ Date _____

GUIDED READING *Watergate: Nixon's Downfall*

As you read about Watergate, answer the questions shown on the following time line.

1972

June   **Break-in at DNC campaign office**   →   1. How were the "plumbers" connected to President Nixon?

Nov.   **Nixon wins reelection.**

1973

Jan.   **Plumbers go on trial.**   →   2. Who was the judge? Why did he hand out maximum sentences?

Mar.   **Mitchell and Dean are implicated.**   →   3. How were Mitchell and Dean connected to Nixon?

April   **Dean is fired; Haldeman and Erlichman resign.**   →   4. How were Haldeman and Erlichman connected to Nixon?

May   **Senate opens Watergate hearings.**   →   5. What did the following men tell the Senate about Nixon?

     a. Dean

     b. Butterfield

Oct.   **Saturday Night Massacre**   →   6. Who was fired or forced to resign in the "massacre"?

1974

April   **Edited transcripts of tapes are released.**   →   7. Why weren't investigators satisfied with the transcripts?

July   **Supreme Court orders surrender of tapes.**

Aug.   **House committee adopts impeachment articles.**

     Unedited tapes are released.   →   8. What did the tapes reveal?

     Nixon resigns.

CHAPTER 24

Section 3

GUIDED READING *The Ford and Carter Years*

A. As you read about Presidents Ford and Carter, take notes to describe the policies of each toward the problems facing them.

Problems Faced by Ford	Policies
1. Ending Watergate scandal	
2. Troubled economy	
3. Hostile Congress	
4. Cold War tensions	
5. Southeast Asia	

Problems Faced by Carter	Policies
6. Distrust of politicians	
7. Energy crisis	
8. Discrimination	
9. Human rights issues	
10. Panama Canal	
11. Cold War tensions	
12. Middle East tensions	

B. On the back of this paper, explain the importance of the **Camp David Accords** and the **Ayatollah Ruhollah Khomeini** to the Carter administration.

Name _____ Date _____

GUIDED READING *Environmental Activism*

CHAPTER 24
Section 4

A. As you read about the nation's efforts to address environmental problems, take notes to describe how American attitudes were affected by each event or how the event affected the environment itself.

Events	Effects on Attitudes or Environment
1. Publication of Rachel Carson's *Silent Spring*	
2. Celebration of Earth Day	
3. Creation of the Environmental Protection Agency	
4. Passage of the new Clean Air Act	
5. Passage of the Alaska Native Claims Settlement Act	
6. Nuclear accident at Three Mile Island	

B. On the back of this paper, define **environmentalist.**

Name _____ Date _____

A. Completion Select the term or name that best completes the sentence.

realpolitik	Lois Gibbs	Jimmy Carter
Rachel Carson	Gerald Ford	New Federalism
détente	Watergate	Saturday Night Massacre

1. President Nixon's plan of distributing a portion of federal power to state and local governments was known as _____.

2. According to the philosophy of _____, foreign policy should be based on consideration of power, not ideals or moral principles.

3. The rapid firing of the U.S. Attorney General and his deputy over the battle for Nixon's Watergate tapes was known as the _____.

4. Shortly after becoming president, _____ pardoned Richard Nixon for his role in the Watergate scandal.

5. With the publication of *Silent Spring*, marine biologist and author _____, helped Americans wake up to the harm they were inflicting on the environment.

B. Evaluating Write *T* in the blank if the statement is true. If the statement is false, write *F* in the blank and then write the corrected statement on the line below.

_____ 1. The scandal known as Watergate centered on the Nixon administration's attempt to cover up a burglary of the Democratic National Committee headquarters.

_____

_____ 2. Stagflation was a combination of high inflation and decreased consumer spending.

_____

_____ 3. The Camp David Accords was a peace agreement forged between Israel and Syria.

_____

_____ 4. The Environmental Protection Agency is the federal government's main instrument for dealing with environmental issues.

_____

_____ 5. Under the SALT I Treaty, the United States and the Soviet Union agreed to destroy all of their intercontinental ballistic missiles and submarine-launched missiles.

_____

C. Writing Write a paragraph describing the Nixon White House using the following terms.

H. R. Haldeman   **John Ehrlichman**   **John Mitchell**

Name _____ Date _____

SKILLBUILDER PRACTICE *Analyzing Assumptions and Biases*

Time *magazine declared the environment the "Issue of the Year" for 1970. Read this excerpt from* Time's *article on the environment. Then fill out the form to help you analyze the article's underlying assumptions. (See Skillbuilder Handbook, p. R15.)*

"The astonishing achievement of the year," says Ecologist Lamont Cole of Cornell, "is that people are finally aware of the size of the problem." They can hardly avoid it. In 1970, the cause that once concerned lonely crusaders like Rachel Carson became a national issue that at times verged on a national obsession: it appealed even to people normally enraged by attacks on the status quo. With remarkable rapidity it became a tenet in the American credo, at least partially uniting disparate public figures ranging from Cesar Chavez to Barry Goldwater and New York's conservative Senator-elect James Buckley.

At the root of this phenomenon were the dire warnings of ecologists that man's heedless outpouring of noxious wastes is overwhelming the biosphere's ability to cleanse itself. . . .

For its part, the U.S. faced hard choices between ecology and economics. President Nixon set the pattern for official action: a zigzag between environmental reforms and worries about the [economic] recession. He supported the SST [a supersonic aircraft that many felt would harm the envi-

ronment], partly to help save 20,000 aerospace jobs, and he ordered more timbering in national forests despite objections of environmentalists and Congressmen. To soothe oil producers, he opened up 543,897 acres in the oil-polluted Gulf of Mexico for oil exploration and drilling.

Conservationists winced when Nixon fired Interior Secretary Walter J. Hickel for his abrasive style and disagreement with Administration policies. Hickel had become the unexpected hero of episodes like the battle to halt a jetport that endangered Florida's Everglades National Park. . . .

In firing Hickel, though, Nixon replaced him with a potentially tougher law enforcer: the new Environmental Protection Agency under William Ruckelshaus. Nixon also named Russell Train, a respected conservationist, to head the Council on Environmental Quality. He proposed an international treaty to control development of the ocean floors, and signed a bill making oil polluters liable for damage.

from *Time* (January 4, 1971), p. 21.

Assumption about pollution:
This assumption is **directly stated** or **implied** (circle one).	It is based on **evidence** or **bias** (circle one).

Assumption about Nixon's policies:
This assumption is **directly stated** or **implied** (circle one).	It is based on **evidence** or **bias** (circle one).

CHAPTER
24
Section 1

RETEACHING ACTIVITY *The Nixon Administration*

Finding Main Ideas

The following questions deal with counterculture movement. Answer them in the space provided.

1. In what ways did Nixon's New Federalism both enhance and hurt federal social programs?

_____

_____

2. What was President Nixon's Southern strategy?

_____

_____

3. Did Richard Nixon help or hinder the civil rights movement? Explain.

_____

_____

4. What steps did President Nixon take against stagflation? What were the results?

_____

_____

5. What effect did realpolitik have on Cold War tensions between the United States and Soviet Union?

_____

_____

6. How did Richard Nixon put the philosophy of realpolitik into action?

_____

_____

Name _____ Date _____

RETEACHING ACTIVITY *Watergate: Nixon's Downfall*

Sequencing

A. Complete the time line below by describing the key events of the Watergate scandal.

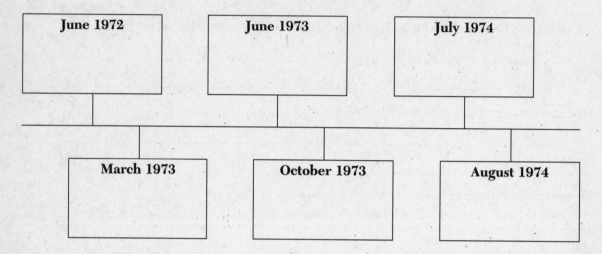

Main Ideas

B. Answer the following questions in the space provided.

1. Why did Vice President Spiro Agnew resign?

_____

_____

2. What did the House Judiciary Committee charge President Nixon with?

_____

_____

3. What was the legacy of Watergate?

_____

_____

CHAPTER 24
Section 3

RETEACHING ACTIVITY *The Ford and Carter Years*

Reading Comprehension

Choose the best answer for each item. Write the letter of your answer in the blank.

_____ 1. The agreements signed during the Ford presidency that promised greater cooperation between
Eastern and Western Europe were known as the
   a. SALT I Treaty.
   b. Geneva Accords.
   c. Helsinki Accords.
   d. Camp David Accords.

_____ 2. The first African American to serve as U.S. ambassador to the United Nations was
   a. Andrew Young.
   b. James Meredith.
   c. A. Philip Randolph.
   d. Thurgood Marshall.

_____ 3. The "moral equivalent of a war" is how President Carter described the nation's battle against
   a. inflation.
   b. unemployment.
   c. the energy crisis.
   d. the Soviet Union.

_____ 4. The 1978 Supreme Court decision that dealt a setback to affirmative action by declaring racial
quotas unconstitutional was
   a. *Mapp v. Ohio.*
   b. *Miranda v. Arizona.*
   c. *Brown v. Board of Education of Topeka.*
   d. *Regents of the University of California v. Bakke.*

_____ 5. U.S. anger over the Soviet Union's invasion of Afghanistan led to the collapse of the
   a. SALT II Treaty.
   b. Geneva Accords.
   c. Helsinki Accords.
   d. Camp David Accords.

_____ 6. In exchange for releasing 52 Americans hostages, revolutionaries in Iran demanded that the
United States
   a. break is alliance with Israel.
   b. remove all troops from the Middle East.
   c. hand over the much-hated shah of Iran.
   d. supply Iran with military and financial aid.

CHAPTER
24
Section 4

RETEACHING ACTIVITY *Environmental Activism*

Matching

A. Match the description in the second column with term in the first column. Write the appropriate letter next to the word.

_____ 1. Rachel Carson

_____ 2. environmentalist

_____ 3. DDT

_____ 4. Three Mile Island

_____ 5. Earth Day

_____ 6. Alaska

a. yearly celebration of the environment

b. site of nuclear disaster 1979

c. wrote Silent Spring

d. site of significant oil discovery in 1968

e. controversial pesticide outlawed in 1972

f. one who works to protect the environment

Evaluating

B. Write *T* in the blank if the statement is true. If the statement is false, write *F* in the blank and then write the corrected statement on the line below it.

_____ 1. The Alaska Native Claims Settlement Act gave Alaska's native tribes millions of dollars in return their land to be used for oil drilling.

_____

_____ 2. During the entire crisis at Three Mile Island, radiation never actually leaked from the reactor.

_____

_____ 3. As a result of the accident at Three Mile Island, the Nuclear Regulatory Commission strengthened its safety standards and improved its inspection procedures.

_____

_____ 4. Americans still celebrate Earth Day each year on September 22.

_____

_____ 5. The publication of *Silent Spring* in 1962 prompted the Kennedy administration to establish a committee to investigate the use of pesticides.

_____

CHAPTER 24

Section 3

GEOGRAPHY APPLICATION: HUMAN–ENVIRONMENT INTERACTION
Oil Consumption in the 1970s

Directions: Read the paragraphs below and study the graphs carefully. Then answer the questions that follow.

In the 1800s, gasoline was considered a useless by-product of oil refining and was often discarded into bodies of water. Kerosene, for burning in lamps, was the main product distilled from oil. In the 1900s, however, technology changed the way oil was used. Electric lighting replaced kerosene lighting, and automobiles and other motor vehicles began creating a need for all of that unwanted gasoline.

Throughout the century the demand for oil increased, and by 1973, 47 percent of U.S. energy consumption from all sources was coming from oil. Nevertheless, supplies were always abundant, so the price of oil stayed low. As demand began to outstrip U.S. production, however, the United States became increasingly dependent on foreign sources for oil.

Then, the United States experienced two oil crises. In 1973–1974, the Arab members of the

Organization of Petroleum Exporting Countries (OPEC), a collective-bargaining group of oil-producing nations, were angry about Western support of Israel during its 1973 war with its Arab neighbors. They cut off oil exports to the United States, and at the same time the other OPEC members raised prices, from about $3 to more than $12 a barrel. U.S. gasoline and heating-oil prices soared. In 1979, OPEC again increased oil prices drastically, and the cost of a barrel of crude oil rose from around $12 to more than $30.

The bar graphs below dramatize how dependent the United States was on foreign oil in the 1970s and how the increased cost of oil affected consumption. Oil consumption is measured in British thermal units (Btu), with 1 Btu being the quantity of heat needed to raise the temperature of one pound of water one degree Fahrenheit. A quadrillion is a million billion.

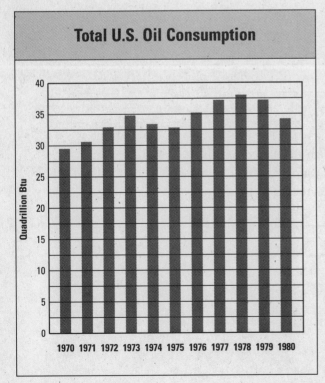

Total U.S. Oil Consumption

(Quadrillion Btu vs. years 1970–1980)

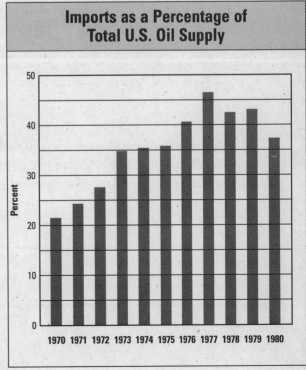

Imports as a Percentage of Total U.S. Oil Supply

(Percent vs. years 1970–1980)

Interpreting Text and Visuals

1. What was the trend in oil consumption from 1970 through 1973? _____

_____

2. How much oil did Americans consume in 1973? _____

3. In which year during the 1970s was oil consumption the greatest? _____

4. Why were there rather sharp declines in oil consumption after 1973 and 1979? _____

_____

_____

5. What do you imagine happened to oil consumption in 1981? Why? _____

_____

_____

_____

6. Logically, why should the percentage of imported oil consumed in the United
   States have dropped in 1973–1974? _____

_____

   Why do you think it did not? _____

_____

_____

7. Until 1969, imported oil had never been more than 19.8 percent of the total
   amount of oil consumed in the United States. In your own words, summarize
   what happened to U.S. reliance on imported oil in the 1970s.

_____

_____

_____

_____

PRIMARY SOURCE Newspaper Front Page

CHAPTER 24
Section 1

On July 20, 1969, about 600 million Americans tuned in to watch a historic event on their TV sets. They witnessed Neil Armstrong step out of the lunar module, the Eagle, and stand on the surface of the moon. Study the headlines from this New York Times *front page to learn more about the first moon walk.*

Activity Options

1. With a partner, use the headlines from this newspaper front page as well as information from your textbook chapters 20 and 24 to re-create a TV broadcast of the moon walk. Act as newscasters who report the event live from earth.

2. Write your own headline about the moon walk that could have been printed on this front page and share it with the class.

CHAPTER 24

Section 2

PRIMARY SOURCE *from All the President's Men*
by Carl Bernstein and Bob Woodward

Washington Post reporters Bob Woodward and Carl Bernstein first broke the Watergate story. As you read this excerpt from their book on the scandal, consider why they made an unlikely team.

June 17, 1972. Nine o'clock Saturday morning. Early for the telephone. Woodward fumbled for the receiver and snapped awake. The city editor of the *Washington Post* was on the line. Five men had been arrested earlier that morning in a burglary at Democratic headquarters, carrying photographic equipment and electronic gear. Could he come in?

Woodward had worked for the *Post* for only nine months and was always looking for a good Saturday assignment, but this didn't sound like one. A burglary at the local Democratic headquarters was too much like most of what he had been doing—investigative pieces on unsanitary restaurants and small-time police corruption. Woodward had hoped he had broken out of that; he had just finished a series of stories on the attempted assassination of Alabama Governor George Wallace. Now, it seemed, he was back in the same old slot.

Woodward left his one-room apartment in downtown Washington and walked the six blocks to the Post. The newspaper's mammoth newsroom—over 150 feet square with rows of brightly colored desks set on an acre of sound-absorbing carpet—is usually quiet on Saturday morning. . . . As Woodward stopped to pick up his mail and telephone messages at the front of the newsroom, he noticed unusual activity around the city desk. He checked in with the city editor and learned with surprise that the burglars had not broken into the small local Democratic Party office but the headquarters of the Democratic National Committee in the Watergate office-apartment-hotel complex. . . .

As Woodward began making phone calls, he noticed that Bernstein, one of the paper's two Virginia political reporters, was working on the burglary story too.

Oh God, not Bernstein, Woodward thought, recalling several office tales about Bernstein's ability to push his way into a good story and get his byline on it.

That morning, Bernstein had Xeroxed copies of notes from reporters at the scene and informed the city editor that he would make some more checks.

The city editor had shrugged his acceptance, and Bernstein had begun a series of phone calls to everybody at the Watergate he could reach—desk clerks, bellmen, maids in the housekeeping department, waiters in the restaurant.

Bernstein looked across the newsroom. There was a pillar between his desk and Woodward's, about 25 feet away. He stepped back several paces. It appeared that Woodward was also working on the story. That figured, Bernstein thought. Bob Woodward was a prima donna who played heavily at office politics. Yale. A veteran of the Navy officer corps. Lawns, greensward, staterooms and grass tennis courts, Bernstein guessed, but probably not enough pavement for him to be good at investigative reporting. Bernstein knew that Woodward couldn't write very well. One office rumor had it that English was not Woodward's native language.

Bernstein was a college dropout. He had started as a copy boy at the *Washington Star* when he was 16, become a full-time reporter at 19, and had worked at the *Post* since 1966. He occasionally did investigative series, had covered the courts and city hall, and liked to do long, discursive pieces about the capital's people and neighborhoods.

Woodward knew that Bernstein occasionally wrote about rock music for the *Post*. That figured. When he learned that Bernstein sometimes reviewed classical music, he choked that down with difficulty. Bernstein looked like one of those counterculture journalists that Woodward despised. Bernstein thought that Woodward's rapid rise at the *Post* had less to do with his ability than his Establishment credentials.

They had never worked on a story together.

from Carl Bernstein and Bob Woodward, *All the President's Men* (New York: Simon and Schuster, 1974), 13–15.

Research Option

Find and read a *Washington Post* article about Watergate that was written by Woodward and Bernstein. Then write a summary of the article.

CHAPTER 24

Section 4

PRIMARY SOURCE *from Love Canal: My Story*
by Lois Gibbs

After discovering that her son's elementary school was built over a toxic waste dump, Lois Gibbs went door-to-door with a petition to see if other parents felt as angry as she did. Read this excerpt to find out about Gibbs's gradual awareness of the environmental crisis brewing in her own backyard.

As I proceeded down 99th Street, I developed a set speech. I would tell people what I wanted. But the speech wasn't all that necessary. It seemed as though every home on 99th Street had someone with an illness. One family had a young daughter with arthritis. They couldn't understand why she had it at her age. Another daughter had had a miscarriage. The father, still a fairly young man, had had a heart attack. I went to the next house, and there, people would tell me their troubles. People were reaching out; they were telling me their troubles in hopes I would do something. But I didn't know anything to do. I was also confused. I just wanted to stop children from going to that school. Now look at all those other health problems! Maybe they were related to the canal. But even if they were, what could I do?

As I continued going door-to-door, I heard more. The more I heard, the more frightened I became. This problem involved much more than the 99th Street School. The entire community seemed to be sick! Then I remembered my own neighbors. One who lived on the left of my husband and me was suffering from severe migraines and had been hospitalized three or four times that year. Her daughter had kidney problems and bleeding. A woman on the other side of us had gastrointestinal problems. A man in the next house down was dying of lung cancer and he didn't even work in industry. The man across the street had just had lung surgery. I thought about Michael; maybe there was more to it than just the school. I didn't understand how chemicals could get all the way over to 101st Street from 99th; but the more I thought about it, the more frightened I became—for my family and for the whole neighborhood. . . .

I continued to go door-to-door. I was becoming more worried because of the many families with children who had birth defects. Then I learned something even more frightening: there had been five crib deaths within a few short blocks.

I was still getting people's cooperation and interest, but I was soon to learn that not everyone

felt the same way I did. The woman on 97th Street who had done some organizing never provided any help. We never argued; in fact, she never said anything. One day, while I was knocking on doors, I noticed her riding on her bicycle. She seemed to be watching me. I was both puzzled and intimidated mainly because my self-confidence wasn't yet all that high. I thought we had a common problem, that we should be working together. But she had tried to organize the neighborhood; therefore, it was her neighborhood, her territory. Maybe she felt I was stepping on her toes.

I finally got up my courage and walked over. "Hi," I said. She was in front of her house. A tree in the front yard was wilted. It looked sick, as though it were dying. We stood in the yard and talked. She told me she couldn't use her backyard, that everything there was dead. She asked what I was doing, and I told her. Her voice suddenly turned cold. She warned me about rocking the boat, telling me not to make waves. She had already taken care of the problem. She had been working hard, talking to a number of politicians, and she didn't want me to undo what she had done.

I was taken aback. I explained that I didn't want to "undo" anything, that I wanted to work *with* her. It was a very hot day. . . . There we were, standing in the hot sun, with the only shade coming from a dying tree, and she was telling me how everything was all right. I didn't know what to think. I had to go home and figure this out. I went home, but not because I was frightened. I just needed time to think, to figure out what was happening.

from Lois Marie Gibbs, *Love Canal: My Story* (Albany: State University of New York Press, 1982), 15–17.

Discussion Questions

1. How did Gibbs's neighbors respond to her when she went door-to-door with a petition?
2. What different health problems did Gibbs's neighbors experience?

Name _____ Date _____

CHAPTER 24

Section 4

PRIMARY SOURCE *from Silent Spring*
by Rachel Carson

Biologist Rachel Carson spent four and a half years gathering data. In Silent
Spring, *she explained how pesticides affect the delicate balance of nature.*

The history of life on earth has been a history of interaction between living things and their surroundings. To a large extent, the physical form and the habits of the earth's vegetation and its animal life have been molded by the environment. Considering the whole span of earthly time, the opposite effect, in which life actually modifies its surroundings, has been relatively slight. Only within the moment of time represented by the present century has one species—man—acquired significant power to alter the nature of his world.

During the past quarter century this power has not only increased to one of disturbing magnitude but it has changed in character. The most alarming of all man's assaults upon the environment is the contamination of air, earth, rivers, and sea with dangerous and even lethal materials. This pollution is for the most part irrecoverable; the chain of evil it initiates not only in the world that must support life but in living tissues is for the most part irreversible. In this now universal contamination of the environment, chemicals are the sinister and little-recognized partners of radiation in changing the very nature of the world—the very nature of its life. . . . Chemicals sprayed on croplands or forests or gardens lie long in soil, entering into living organisms, passing from one to another in a chain of poisoning and death. Or they pass mysteriously by underground streams until they emerge and, through the alchemy of air and sunlight, combine into new forms that kill vegetation, sicken cattle, and work unknown harm on those who drink from once pure wells. As Albert Schweitzer has said, "Man can hardly even recognize the devils of his own creation."

It took hundreds of millions of years to produce the life that now inhabits the earth—eons of time in which that developing and evolving and diversifying life reached a state of adjustment and balance with its surroundings. The environment, rigorously shaping and directing the life it supported, contained elements that were hostile as well as supporting. Certain rocks gave out dangerous radiation; even within the light of the sun, from which all life draws its energy, there were short-wave radiations with power to injure. Given time—time not in years but in millennia—life adjusts, and a balance has been reached. For time is the essential ingredient; but in the modern world there is no time.

The rapidity of change and the speed with which new situations are created follow the impetuous and heedless pace of man rather than the deliberate pace of nature. . . . The chemicals to which life is asked to make its adjustment are no longer merely the calcium and silica and copper and all the rest of the minerals washed out of the rocks and carried in rivers to the sea; they are the synthetic creations of man's inventive mind, brewed in his laboratories, and having no counterparts in nature.

To adjust to these chemicals would require time on the scale that is nature's; it would require not merely the years of a man's life but the life of generations. And even this, were it by some miracle possible, would be futile, for the new chemicals come from our laboratories in an endless stream; almost five hundred annually find their way into actual use in the United States alone. . . .

These sprays, dusts, and aerosols are now applied almost universally to farms, gardens, forests, and homes—nonselective chemicals that have the power to kill every insect, the "good" and the "bad," to still the song of birds and the leaping of fish in the streams, to coat the leaves with a deadly film, and to linger on in soil—all this though the intended target may be only a few weeds or insects. Can anyone believe it is possible to lay down such a barrage of poisons on the surface of the earth without making it unfit for all life? They should not be called "insecticides," but "biocides."

from Rachel Carson, *Silent Spring* (New York: Houghton Mifflin, 1962), 5–8.

Research Options

1. Find out about pesticides that are currently in use in the United States.
2. Find out about alternatives to pesticide use in controlling insects and rodents.

CHAPTER 24

Section 3

LITERATURE SELECTION *from* **Memories of the Ford Administration** by John Updike

This novel's main character, Alfred Clayton, receives a request from the Northern New England Association of American Historians (NNEAAH) to share his impressions of Gerald Ford's administration. He weaves together his impressions of the politics of the time with memories of events in his own life. As you read this excerpt, think about whether Clayton's impressions of the Ford administration are positive or negative.

From: Alfred L. Clayton, A.B. '58, Ph.D. '62

To: Northern New England Association of American Historians, Putney, Vermont

Re: Requested Memories and Impressions of the Presidential Administration of Gerald R. Ford (1974–77), for Written Symposium on Same to Be Published in NNEAAH's Triquarterly Journal, *Retrospect*

I remember I was sitting among my abandoned children watching when Nixon resigned. My wife was out on a date, and had asked me to babysit. We had been separated since June. This was, of course, August. Nixon, with his bulgy face and his menacing, slipped-cog manner, seemed about to cry. The children and I had never seen a President resign before; nobody in the history of the United States had ever seen that.

Our impressions—well, who can tell what the impressions of children are? Andrew was fifteen, Buzzy just thirteen, Daphne a plump and vulnerable eleven. For them, who had been historically conscious ten years at the most, this resignation was not so epochal, perhaps. The late Sixties and early Seventies had produced so much in the way of bizarre headlines and queer television that they were probably less struck than I was. Spiro Agnew had himself resigned not many months before; Gerald Ford was thus our only non-elected President, unless you count Joe Tumulty in the wake of Wilson's stroke or James G. Blaine during the summer when poor Garfield was being slowly slain by the medical science of 1881, . . .

[W]as there ever a Ford Administration? Evidence for its existence seems to be scanty. I have been doing some sneak objective research, though you ask for memories and impressions, both subjective. The hit songs of the years 1974–76 apparently were

"Seasons in the Sun"
"The Most Beautiful Girl"
"The Streak"
"Please, Mister Postman"
"Mandy"
"Top of the World"
"Just You and Me"
"Rhinestone Cowboy"
"Fame"
"Best of My Love"
"Laughter in the Rain"
"The Hustle"
"Have You Never Been Mellow?"
"One of These Nights"
"Jive Talkin'"
"Silly Love Songs"
"Black Water"
"Don't Go Breakin' My Heart"
"Play That Funky Music"
"A Fifth of Beethoven"
"Shake Your Booty"
"Breaking Up Is Hard to Do"
"Love Is Alive"
"Sara Smile"
"Get Closer"

I don't recall hearing any of them. Whenever I turned on the radio, WADM was pouring out J. S. Bach's merry tintinnabulations or the surging cotton candy of P. I. Tchaikovsky, the inventor of sound-track music. No, wait—"Don't Go Breakin' My Heart" rings a faint bell, I can almost hum it, and the same goes for "Breaking Up Is Hard to Do," if it's not the same song. In fact, all twenty-five titles give me the uneasy sensation of being the same song. The top non-fiction bestsellers of those years were *All the President's Men, More Joy: Lovemaking Companion to the Joy of Sex, You Can Profit from a Monetary Crisis, Angels: God's Secret Agents, Winning Through Intimidation, Sylvia Porter's Money Book, Total Fitness in 30 Minutes a*

Week, Blind Ambition: The White House Years, The Grass Is Always Greener over the Septic Tank, and *The Hite Report:* I read none of them. Fiction, too, evaded my ken; the multitudes but not I revelled in the dramatized information of such chunky, universal titles as *Jaws, Shogun, Ragtime, Trinity, Centennial,* and *1876,* or in the wistful escapism of *All Things Bright and Beautiful* and *Watership Down,* which was, I seem very imperfectly to recall, somehow about rabbits. The top TV shows were *All in the Family, Happy Days,* and *Laverne and Shirley:* I never watched them, having no TV set in my furtive digs. I would half-hear the interrupting news bulletins on WADM whenever some woman would take a shot at Ford or Ford took a shot at the Cambodians—Cambodia being the heart of the world's darkness in these years—but otherwise the only news that concerned me was what came over the telephone and up the stairs. . . .

The last thing I remember about the Ford Administration is sitting with my children watching, while a New England January held us snug indoors, a youngish-seeming man walking down Pennsylvania Avenue with one hand in his wife's and the other waving to the multitudes. Washington City was bathed in telegenic white sunlight and Carter was hatless, in pointed and rather embarrassing echo of Kennedy fourteen years and four Presidents ago. A hundred years after the end of Reconstruction and the one indisputably fraudulent Presidential election in American history, a son of the South had risen, without benefit of (cf. Truman, Tyler, and the two Johnsons) another President's demise. The youngish, hatless man's smile was broad and constant but not, absolutely, convincing; we were in a time, as in the stretch between Polk and Lincoln, of unconvincing Presidents. But Polk and Lincoln, too, had their doubters and mockers and haters by the millions; perhaps it lies among the President's many responsibilities to be unconvincing, to set before us, at an apex of visibility, an illustration of how far short of perfection must fall even the most conscientious application to duty and

> *However much Carter wanted to be liked, we could not quite like him: the South couldn't quite like him because he was liberal and an engineer, the Northeast liberals couldn't because he was a Southerner and a born-again Christian.*

the most cunning solicitation of selfish interests, throwing us back upon the essential American axiom that no divinely appointed leader will save us, we must do it on our own. Of all the forty-odd, handsome Warren Harding was in a sense the noblest, for only he, upon being notified that he had done a bad job, had the grace to die of a broken heart.

In the three fuzzy heads around me—no, I miscounted, there can be only two, Andy is off at college by January of 1977, he is eighteen and in his freshman year; he chose to go to Duke, to put a bit of distance between himself and his wayward parents—there was, if I can be trusted to read the minds of children, a dubiety not unlike my own at the sunny spectacle being beamed to us from the District of Columbia. No other President had ever seen fit to walk back from the inauguration to the White House. It made him, we felt, a bit too much like the circus clown who, with painted smile, jesting now in this direction and now in that, leads the parade into the big tent—the acrobats and the jugglers, the solemn elephants of foreign policy and the caged tigers of domestic distress.

"Showoff," Buzzy said, in his manly baritone, which I was still not quite used to.

"Suppose he gets shot?" Daphne asked. She had been in my lap, up in our apple-green home at Dartmouth, a few months old, the Sunday that Lee Harvey Oswald had been plugged for his sins on national television. She had been weaned, you might say, on assassination.

However much Carter wanted to be liked, we could not quite like him: the South couldn't quite like him because he was a liberal and an engineer, the Northeast liberals couldn't because he was a Southerner and a born-again Christian, the Christians were put off because he had told *Playboy* [magazine] he had *looked upon a lot of women with lust,* and the common masses because his lips were too fat and he talked like a squirrel nibbling an acorn. Blacks liked him, those blacks who still took any interest in the national establishment, but this worked in his disfavor, since the blacks were more and more seen as citizens of a floating Welfare State concealed within the other fifty, and whose settled purpose and policy was to steal money from hard-working taxpayers. Carter and the other liberal Democrats were white accomplices to this theft, this free ride. Furthermore he told us things we didn't want to hear: We should turn our thermostats down and our other cheek to the Iranians. Our hearts were full of lust, we were suffering from a malaise. All true, but truth isn't what we want from Presidents. We have historians for that.

Forgive me, NNEAAH, and editors of *Retrospect;* I've not forgotten it was Ford you requested my impressions of, not Carter. But what did Ford *do?* As I've said, I was preoccupied by personal affairs, and had the radio in my little apartment turned to WADM—all classical, with newsbreaks on the hour of only a minute or two. As far as I could tell, Ford was doing everything right—he got the *Mayaguez* back from the Cambodians, evacuated from Vietnam our embassy staff and hangers-on (literally: there were pictures of people clinging to the helicopter skids in the newsmagazines in my dentist's office), went to Helsinki to meet Brezhnev and sign some peaceable accords, slowly won out over inflation and recession, restored confidence in the Presidency, and pardoned Nixon, which saved the nation a mess of recrimination and legal expense. As far as I know, he was perfect, which can be said of no other President since James Monroe. Further, he was the only President to preside with a name completely different from the one he was given at birth— Leslie King, Jr. "President King" would have been an awkward oxymoron.

There was a picturesque little layer of snow in Washington on television, so there must have been mounds of it in New Hampshire, and ice in the river, black and creaky, and bare twigs making a lace at the windows. Twigs. Our nest. Where was [my wife,] Norma? My still regnant Queen of Disorder? Not within the frame of this memory, somehow. She could have been painting in her alluringly odoriferous studio, or drifting through one of her do-it-yourself lectures on art appreciation over at the college, but my memory places her in the kitchen, tossing together a meal for us all. But wait—the 20th of January was a Thursday, according to my perpetual calendar, so Buzzy and Daphne must have been at school, puzzling their way through the post-noon lessons, or gobbling up the beef-barley soup and American chop suey the school cafeteria provides on Thursdays. Perhaps we were all watching Carter's stroll on the evening-news rerun, and Norma was in the kitchen, cooking our dinner. She wandered in to join us. She held against the bib of her apron a curved wooden sculpting tool, with a serrated edge, that she used as a stew stirrer. She looked over our shoulders and said, "After Watergate, I don't see how the Republicans will ever elect another President."

Discussion Questions

1. What is Clayton's first memory of the Ford administration?
2. What is his last memory?
3. What does Clayton's objective research on popular culture during the Ford administration turn up?
4. Based on your reading of this excerpt, how would you characterize Clayton's overall assessment of the Ford administration?

Name _____ Date _____

AMERICAN LIVES # Henry Kissinger
Secretly Seeking Shared Interests

"In a democracy the results of negotiations obviously have to be made available to the public. . . . The process by which these results are achieved generally should have a private phase."—Henry Kissinger in an interview with American Heritage *magazine (1983)*

Henry Kissinger was the first foreign-born person to serve as the U.S. Secretary of State. He achieved this high position through his skill at diplomacy.

Kissinger was born in Germany in 1923. Increasingly threatened after the Nazis took control in 1933, his family fled to the United States in 1938. He joined the army in 1943 and fought in the closing years of the war in Europe. Back in the United States after the war, Kissinger attended college and graduate school. He began to teach and write on defense issues. An early book introduced the idea of "flexible response." This idea rejected the 1950s policy of reliance on nuclear weapons for national defense. He argued that the United States should, instead, build conventional forces to be able to defend itself without nuclear weapons. President Kennedy adopted the policy.

After his election as president in 1968, Richard Nixon named Kissinger as his national security advisor. The post gave Kissinger daily access to the president and broad authority to carry out Nixon's new foreign policy ideas. The two worked together very closely. Kissinger launched talks with the Soviet Union to limit nuclear weapons. His secret visits to China and the Soviet Union paved the way for Nixon's historic visits. Secret talks with North Vietnam paved the way for the end of U.S. involvement in Vietnam, and he shared the Nobel Peace Prize in 1973 with Le Duc Tho, a North Vietnamese diplomat. In that year he helped negotiate a halt to fighting in the Middle East.

When Nixon resigned over the Watergate scandal, Kissinger—now secretary of state—stayed in office to serve President Gerald Ford. He returned to the Middle East countless times, using "shuttle diplomacy" to persuade Israel and Egypt to take some early steps toward peace. His efforts also established close American ties with Egypt. Negotiations with the Soviet Union reached another arms control agreement.

Kissinger has said that successful diplomacy has two keys. One is secrecy. It is important, he believes, for diplomats to meet privately so they can explore possible solutions to a problem without heated public debate. The other is that an agreement must benefit both sides. "Nobody," he warns, "will sign an agreement that is exclusively in the other party's interest."

Kissinger has won wide praise—and criticism. Some criticized him for supporting the invasion of Cambodia and other aggressive acts during the Vietnam War. Others said that his agreements with the Soviet Union were too generous to the Soviets. Many critics focused on how far he went to ensure secrecy. When newspapers published secret government information, Kissinger was angered. He agreed to a Nixon administration plan to tap the telephone of his aides to see if they were responsible for the information reaching the papers. Critics said that the newspapers were simply pursuing the people's right to know and that the wiretaps violated the aides' rights.

In 1977 Kissinger retired as secretary of state and received the Presidential Medal of Freedom, the nation's highest civilian honor. In 1982 he formed an international business consulting company. On occasion, however, he has worked on assignments for the government. In 1983, he headed a commission analyzing U.S. policy in Central America. Four years later, he led a team that discussed arms control with the Soviet Union.

Questions

1. Do you think a democracy should be totally open or can it maintain secrecy?
2. Anyone, Kissinger once said, can criticize an agreement between nations on the grounds that the other nation gains something. The key to a good agreement is what your own nation gains in return. Do you agree or disagree? Explain.
3. Should newspapers have been allowed to publish secret information? Explain.

CHAPTER 24

Section 2

AMERICAN LIVES **Barbara Jordan**

Brilliant Speaker, Able Legislator

"We are a people in search of a national community, attempting to fulfill our national purpose, to create and sustain a society in which all of us are equal."
—Barbara Jordan, keynote speech to the Democratic National Convention (1976)

Barbara Jordan (1936–1996) impressed millions of Americans with the eloquence of her words. She impressed colleagues inside the legislatures where she served with her ability to get things done.

At age 16, Jordan won a national contest in speechmaking. She later led her college debating team to a number of championships. After graduating from law school, she returned to Texas and opened a private practice. Soon, Jordan became involved in politics. In 1960, she organized a get-out-the-vote drive that won an unprecedented 80-percent turnout among black voters in her home county. She twice lost races for the Texas House of Representatives. In 1966, however, she won election to the Texas Senate—the first African American elected since 1883 and the first woman ever.

In the Senate, Jordan quickly won admiration for her intelligence and her political skills. She did not want to change the Senate's ways, she said, but to get things done. She pushed the Senate to pass new laws protecting the environment, setting a minimum wage, and fighting job discrimination. In her six years in the Senate, half the bills she introduced became law.

In 1972, Jordan won a seat in the U.S. House of Representatives. Two years later, she rose to national attention. She was part of the Judiciary Committee that debated whether to impeach President Richard Nixon for his involvement in the cover-up of the Watergate affair. Jordan's speech—televised live across the nation—was powerful. She pointed out that as an African-American woman she had not originally been "included" in the Constitution. Now, she said, she was included. Then she vowed, "I am not going to sit here and be an idle spectator in . . . the destruction of the Constitution."

Her speechmaking ability brought her fame again two years later. Her keynote address at the 1976 Democratic National Convention electrified the crowd. Many called for her to be named as the party's vice-presidential candidate. Later that year,

a magazine surveyed Americans to find who they would most like to see as the first woman president. Jordan's name topped the list.

Jordan transferred her success in the Texas legislature to the national Congress. She worked for education and the environment, racial justice, and economic opportunity. Many people were dismayed in 1979 when she retired from the House. She became a teacher at the University of Texas, where her courses in policy and political ethics were always in demand.

Though Jordan no longer held elected office, she continued to speak out on issues that she cared about. She helped start a group that backed liberal causes. She served as a special advisor to the governor of Texas on ethics in government and chaired a presidential commission that studied immigration.

Jordan suffered many illnesses in her later years, but the magic and power of her voice continued. Speaking from a wheelchair, she brought the crowd to its feet at the Democrats' 1992 convention. In 1994 she testified in Congress about a new immigration law. "I would be the last person to claim that our nation is perfect," she said. "but we have a kind of perfection in us because our founding principle is universal—that we are all created equal regardless of race, religion, or national ancestry." That same year Jordan received the Presidential Medal of Freedom, the nation's highest civilian honor.

Questions

1. What did Jordan mean by saying that our "national purpose" was to "create and sustain a society in which all of us are equal"?
2. Was Jordan an effective lawmaker? Explain your answer.
3. Why did Jordan say, in 1974, that she would not allow the Constitution to be destroyed?

Name _____ Date _____

GUIDED READING *A Conservative Movement Emerges*

CHAPTER
25
Section 1

A. As you read about the conservative movement that swept the country, note the individuals, groups, and institutions that fueled it. Then identify issues the New Right emphasized as well as the interests it promoted.

1. Individuals	2. Groups and institutions

3. Issues and interests

B. Identify four factors that contributed to Ronald Reagan's victory.

1.	3.
2.	4.

C. On the back of this paper, define **entitlement program** and **reverse discrimination.**

CHAPTER 25

Section 2

GUIDED READING *Conservative Policies Under Reagan and Bush*

A. As you read, note the results of "Reaganomics" and of actions taken to achieve important goals of the conservative movement.

Goal: Stimulate the economy

1. Cut government spending on social programs and lowered income taxes	→ Result(s):
2. Increased military spending	→ Result(s):

Goal: Promote traditional values and morality

3. Named conservative judges to the Supreme Court and other federal courts	→ Result(s):

Goal: Reduce the size and power of the federal government

5. Cut the Environmental Protection Agency budget and appointed EPA administrators sympathetic to business	→ Result(s):

B. On the back of this paper, define **supply-side economics.** Then identify **Sandra Day O'Connor, William Rehnquist,** and **Geraldine Ferraro.**

CHAPTER

25

Section 3

GUIDED READING *Social Concerns of the 1980s*

A. As you read, identify specific issues in each of the following areas that concerned Americans in the 1980s.

1. Health	2. Education	3. Cities

B. Take notes about the gains, losses, and chief concerns of each of the following groups.

1. Women	2. African Americans	3. Latinos
4. Native Americans	5. Asian Americans	6. Gays and lesbians

C. On the back of this paper, note what **L. Douglas Wilder** and **Jesse Jackson** did to advance African Americans politically.

CHAPTER 25

Section 4

GUIDED READING *Foreign Policy After the Cold War*

As you read about the end of the Cold War, note key persons, events, and trends involved in the nations listed below. Concentrate on political and economic developments as well as on U.S. relations with those countries. Leave the shaded boxes blank.

Nations	Key Individuals	Key Events and Trends
1. Soviet Union		Events: Trends:
2. Poland		Events: Trends:
3. Germany		Events: Trends:
4. Yugoslavia		Events: Trends:
5. China		Events: Trends:
6. Nicaragua		Events: Trends:
7. Panama		Events: Trends:
8. Iran		
9. Iraq		

CHAPTER 25

BUILDING VOCABULARY *The Conservative Tide*

A. Multiple Choice Circle the letter before the term or name that best completes the sentence.

1. Televangelist Jerry Falwell formed the organization known as the (a) New Right (b) Moral Majority (c) conservative coalition.

2. Sandra Day O'Connor was the first woman to be appointed to the (a) Supreme Court (b) cabinet (c) federal bench.

3. Ronald Reagan's successor was (a) Jimmy Carter (b) Colin Powell (c) George H.W. Bush.

4. The nation's first African American governor was (a) Jesse Jackson (c) Colin Powell (c) L. Douglas Wilder.

5. The anti-Communist guerrilla forces in Nicaragua backed by the United States were known as the (a) *Contras* (b) *Sandinistas* (c) *perestroika*.

B. Matching Match the description in the second column with the term or name in the first column. Write the appropriate letter next to the word.

_____ 1. Tiananmen Square   a. guaranteed benefits to particular groups

_____ 2. Strategic Defense Initiative b. effort to liberate Kuwait from Iraqi control

_____ 3. Geraldine Ferraro   c. Russian term meaning *openness*

_____ 4. Lauro Cavazos   d. proposed missile defense system

_____ 5. reverse discrimination   e. site of bloody clash in China

_____ 6. Operation Desert Storm   f. favoring groups on the basis of race or gender

_____ 7. *glasnost*   g. ran for vice-president in 1988

_____ 8. entitlement programs   h. secretary of education under first Bush

C. Writing Write a paragraph about Ronald Reagan's major domestic goals using the following terms.

Reaganomics   **supply-side economics**   **deregulation**

Name _____   Date _____

CHAPTER
25

Section 4

SKILLBUILDER PRACTICE *Analyzing Political Cartoons*

*Political cartoons are cartoons that use humor to make a serious point. They nor-
mally address political matters and other issues of national interest. Political cartoons seek to convey the main point of what are often complex matters in a
concise and straightforward manner. Thus, the ability to analyze political cartoons and determine their message will help you to better understand significant events about which you read. Below is a political cartoon regarding the
Iran-Contra scandal. Examine the cartoon and then answer the questions that
follow. (See Skillbuilder Handbook, p. R24.)*

1. Who is the person pictured in the television? What does presence on the television signify?

_____

2. Who is the person standing to the right?

_____

3. What is the main message of the cartoon?

_____

CHAPTER
25
Section 1

RETEACHING ACTIVITY *A Conservative Movement Emerges*

Completion

A. Complete the chart below by defining each group and summarizing their views.

New Right	Conservative Coalition	Moral Majority
Definition:	Definition:	Definition:
Views:	Views:	Views:

Main Ideas

B. Answer the following questions in the space provided.

1. What jobs did Ronald Reagan hold before running for president?

_____

_____

2. What issues in the 1980 presidential election hurt President Carter

_____

_____

3. Why was Ronald Reagan known as the Great Communicator?

_____

_____

CHAPTER 25

Section 2

RETEACHING ACTIVITY *Conservative Policies Under Reagan and Bush*

Finding Main Ideas

The following questions deal with counterculture movement. Answer them in the space provided.

1. What were the three goals of "Reaganomics"?

_____

_____

2. How did President Reagan's budget cuts hurt the economically depressed members of society?

_____

_____

3. What factors led to the nation's recovery from the recession of the early 1980s?

_____

_____

4. How did the appointments by Reagan and Bush impact the Supreme Court?

_____

_____

5. Why was the Reagan administration viewed as anti-environmentalist?

_____

_____

6. Who made up Ronald Reagan's 1984 coalition and why?

_____

_____

CHAPTER 25

Section 3

RETEACHING ACTIVITY *Social Concerns in the 1980s*

Reading Comprehension

Choose the best answer for each item. Write the letter of your answer in the blank.

_____ 1. In an attempt to improve education in America, a federal commission in 1983 recommend-
ed all of the following except
a. more homework.
b. longer school days.
c. shorter lunch periods.
d. an extended school year.

_____ 2. The city that exploded in racial violence in 1992 after the acquittal of white police officers
accused of beating an African-American man was
a. Chicago.
b. Los Angeles.
c. New York City.
d. Miami.

_____ 3. The nation's fastest growing minority during the 1980s were
a. Latinos.
b. Asians.
c. Africans.
d. Native Americans.

_____ 4. Perhaps the nation's most prominent health epidemic during the 1980s was
a. AIDS.
b. hepatitis.
c. tuberculosis.
d. chronic fatigue syndrome.

_____ 5. The African American leader who ran for Democratic presidential nomination in 1984 and
1988 was
a. L. Douglas Wilder.
b. Jesse Jackson.
c. Andrew Young.
d. Colin Powell.

_____ 6. The operating of gambling casinos was a significant way of bringing in money for
a. Latinos.
b. Asian Americans.
c. African Americans.
d. Native Americans.

Name _____   Date _____

Completion

A. Complete each sentence with the appropriate term or name.

Watergate   Jordan
Berlin Wall   Grenada
Panama   Commonwealth of Independent States
Kuwait   Iran-Contra

1. In 1989, the people of Berlin tore down the _____, one of the most prominent symbols of the Cold War.

2. The Reagan administration scandal involving the sale of arms to Iran and using the money to fund anti-Communist forces in Nicaragua was known as the _____ affair.

3. The Persian Gulf War involved a U.S.-led effort to liberate _____ from Iraq.

4. As the Soviet Union collapsed, the countries once under its control became known as the _____.

5. The United States took military action in _____ to help oust its corrupt leader, General Manuel Antonio Noriega.

Evaluating

B. Write *T* in the blank if the statement is true. If the statement is false, write *F* in the blank and then write the corrected statement on the line below it.

_____ 1. As part of his perestroika plan, Mikhail Gorbachev called for greater government control of the economy.

_____

_____ 2. The protestors at Tiananmen Square were mainly university students who demanded freedom of speech and a greater voice in government.

_____

_____ 3. The Boland Amendment banned military aid to Panama for two years.

_____

_____ 4. As the world's remaining superpower, the United States acted alone in liberating Kuwait from Iraq.

_____

_____ 5. In 1983, U.S. forces invaded the tiny Caribbean island of Grenada to overthrow its pro-Cuban government.

_____

CHAPTER 25

Section 3

GEOGRAPHY APPLICATION: REGION

Latino Population in the 1980s

Directions: Read the paragraphs below and study the graph and the map carefully. Then answer the questions that follow.

Between 1980 and 1990, the Latino population in the United States increased by about 53 percent—from 14.6 million to nearly 22.4 million—as compared to only a 6.7 percent increase by non-Latinos. By 1990, in fact, California's Latino population of nearly 7.7 million ranked higher than the total populations of all but nine states. At current rates of growth, the Latino population in the United States will double by the year 2020, whereas it will take the non-Latino population more than 150 years to double.

Some states have concentrations of Latinos of particular national backgrounds—Mexican in California and Texas, Puerto Rican in New York and New Jersey, and Cuban in Florida, for example.

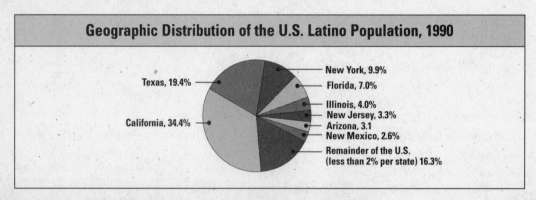

Geographic Distribution of the U.S. Latino Population, 1990

- Texas, 19.4%
- California, 34.4%
- New York, 9.9%
- Florida, 7.0%
- Illinois, 4.0%
- New Jersey, 3.3%
- Arizona, 3.1
- New Mexico, 2.6%
- Remainder of the U.S. (less than 2% per state) 16.3%

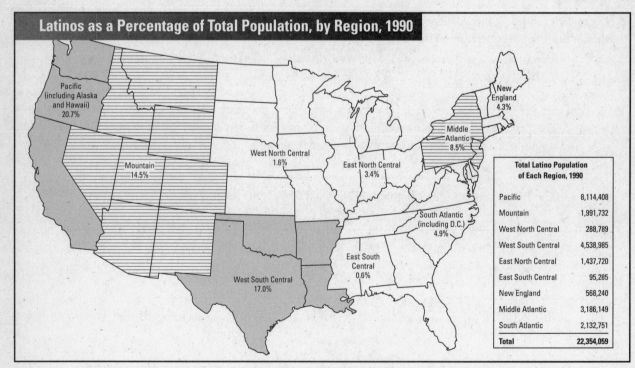

Latinos as a Percentage of Total Population, by Region, 1990

- Pacific (including Alaska and Hawaii) 20.7%
- New England 4.3%
- Middle Atlantic 8.5%
- West North Central 1.6%
- East North Central 3.4%
- Mountain 14.5%
- South Atlantic (including D.C.) 4.9%
- East South Central 0.6%
- West South Central 17.0%

Total Latino Population of Each Region, 1990	
Pacific	8,114,408
Mountain	1,991,732
West North Central	288,789
West South Central	4,538,985
East North Central	1,437,720
East South Central	95,285
New England	568,240
Middle Atlantic	3,186,149
South Atlantic	2,132,751
Total	**22,354,059**

Interpreting Text and Visuals

1. What does "Texas, 19.4%" mean on the pie graph? _____

_____

2. Into how many regions is the U.S. map divided? _____

What does "Middle Atlantic 8.5%" mean on the map? _____

_____

3. In the table to the right of the map, what does the number 1,437,720 mean for
East North Central? _____

_____

4. How many states contained less than 2 percent of the U.S. Latino population
in 1990? _____

Which state contained nearly 10 percent of the Latino population? _____

5. In which region was the percentage of Latinos the smallest?_____

6. Which two states together accounted for more than half of the nation's Latino
population? _____

7. How did the Mountain region rank among all regions in terms of its percentage
of Latinos? How did it rank in terms of its total Latino population? Explain why
the two rankings are not the same.

_____

_____

_____

8. Use your knowledge of geography and economics to suggest reasons for the large
Latino populations in the Southwest, in Florida, and in certain states of the middle
Atlantic region and east north central regions.

_____

_____

_____

_____

CHAPTER 25

Section 4

OUTLINE MAP *U.S. Attention on the Middle East*

A. Review the map "Middle East, 1978–1982" on page 816 of your textbook. To locate some of the African countries not shown on that map and to check for boundary changes in the Gulf of Aden region, also consult the current map of the Middle East on page A16. Then, on the accompanying outline map, label the following bodies of water, countries, and regions (U.A.E. stands for "United Arab Emirates") and draw in the Suez Canal. Use arrows to indicate smaller nations and regions if necessary.

Bodies of Water	Countries			Regions
Arabian Sea	Egypt	Syria	Yemen	West Bank
Caspian Sea	Sudan	Lebanon	Bahrain	Sinai Peninsula
Mediterranean Sea	Eritrea	Israel	Qatar	
Strait of Hormuz	Djibouti	Iraq	Iran	
Persian Gulf	Somalia	Jordan	Saudi Arabia	
Red Sea	Greece	Cyprus	Kuwait	
Gulf of Aden	Turkey	U.A.E.	Oman	

B. After completing the map, use it to answer the following questions.

1. Describe the route a ship leaving a port in Greece would likely take to reach

   Kuwait. _____

2. Which countries have Persian Gulf coastlines? _____

   _____

3. Which country has the longest Red Sea coastline? _____

4. To which nation does the Sinai Peninsula belong? _____

5. Which two labeled countries are islands? _____

6. Which two labeled countries, sharing a common border, are almost totally

   landlocked—that is, without any coastline? _____

7. The Middle East is not a continent but a large region covering parts of three continents. The region is generally considered to consist of Bahrain, Cyprus, Egypt, Iran, Iraq, Israel, Jordan, Kuwait, Lebanon, Oman, Qatar, Saudi Arabia, Sudan, Syria, Turkey, United Arab Emirates, and Yemen. In which three continents are these countries located? Which two countries do you think include parts of two continents? _____

   _____

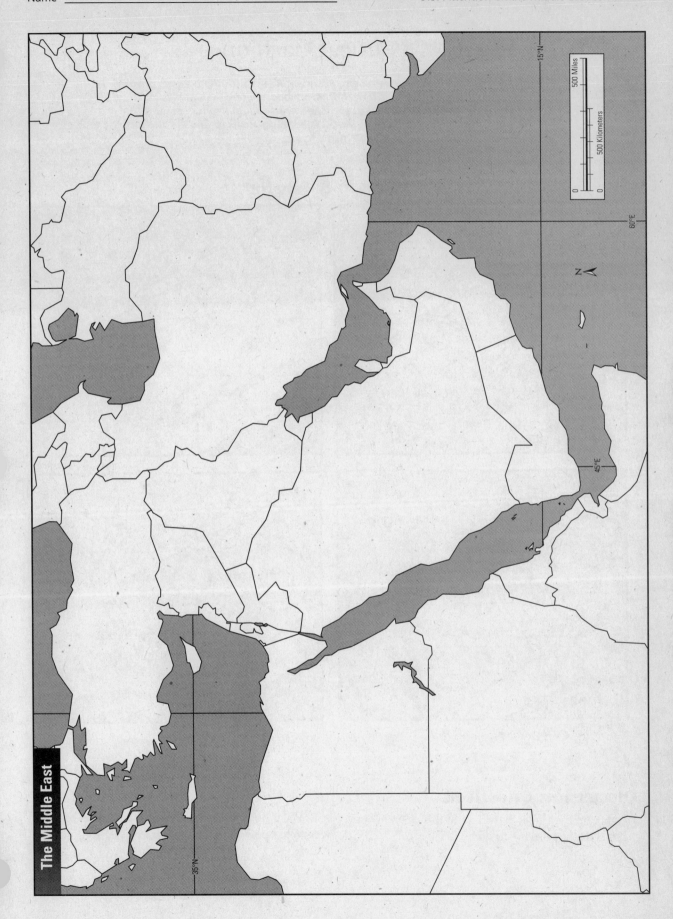

The Middle East

PRIMARY SOURCE Political Cartoon

CHAPTER
25
Section 2

To downsize the federal government, President Reagan cut the budgets of social programs such as urban mass transit, food stamps, welfare, and Medicaid. These programs represented part of the safety net, or minimum financial security, for the poor. Study this cartoon from the St. Petersburg Times to find out the cartoonist's opinion of Reagan's strategy.

The Reagan Safety Net

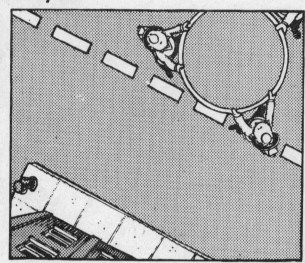

H. CLAY BENNETT
Courtesy St. Petersburg Times

Discussion Questions

1. Who are the three characters in this cartoon, and what are they trying to do?

2. What does the last frame of the cartoon reveal?
3. What political message does this cartoon send?

CHAPTER **25**

Section 2

PRIMARY SOURCE *from* Ronald Reagan's Farewell Address

On January 11, 1989, President Reagan delivered his 34th—and last—address from the Oval Office. As you read this excerpt, think about his assessment of the United States as he prepares to step down after eight years in office.

You know, down the hall and up the stairs from this office is the part of the White House where the president and his family live. There are a few favorite windows I have up there that I like to stand and look out of early in the morning. The view is over the grounds here to the Washington Monument, and then the Mall and the Jefferson Memorial. But on mornings when the humidity is low, you can see past the Jefferson to the river, the Potomac, and the Virginia shore. Someone said that's the view Lincoln had when he saw the smoke rising from the Battle of Bull Run. I see more prosaic things: the grass on the banks, the morning traffic as people make their way to work, now and then a sailboat on the river.

I've been thinking a bit at that window. I've been reflecting what the past eight years have meant and mean. And the image that comes to mind like a refrain is a nautical one—a small story about a big ship, and a refugee and a sailor. It was back in the early eighties, at the height of the boat people. And the sailor was hard at work on the carrier *Midway*, which was patrolling the South China Sea. The sailor, like most American servicemen, was young, smart, and fiercely observant. The crew spied on the horizon a leaky little boat. And crammed inside were refugees from Indochina hoping to get to America. The *Midway* sent a small launch to bring them to the ship and safety. As the refugees made their way through the choppy seas, one spied the sailor on deck and stood up and called out to him. He yelled, "Hello, American sailor. Hello, freedom man."

A small moment with a big meaning, a moment the sailor, who wrote it in a letter, couldn't get out of his mind. And when I saw it, neither could I. Because that's what it was to be an American in the 1980s. We stood, again, for freedom. I know we always have, but in the past few years the world again, and in a way, we ourselves—rediscovered it.

It's been quite a journey this decade, and we held together through some stormy seas. And at

the end, together, we are reaching our destination.

The fact is, from Grenada to the Washington and Moscow summits, from the recession of '81 to '82, to the expansion that began in late '82 and continues to this day, we've made a difference. The way I see it, there were two great triumphs, two things that I'm proudest of. One is the economic recovery, in which the people of America created—and filled—19 million new jobs. The other is the recovery of our morale. America is respected again in the world and looked to for leadership. . . .

The past few days when I've been at that window upstairs, I've thought a bit of the "shining city upon a hill." The phrase comes from John Winthrop, who wrote it to describe the America he imagined. What he imagined was important because he was an early Pilgrim, an early freedom man. He journeyed here on what today we'd call a little wooden boat; and like the other Pilgrims, he was looking for a home that would be free. . . .

And how stands the city on this winter night? More prosperous, more secure, and happier than it was eight years ago. But more than that; after two hundred years, two centuries, she still stands strong and true on the granite ridge, and her glow has held steady no matter what storm. And she's still a beacon, still a magnet for all who must have freedom, for all the pilgrims from all the lost places who are hurtling through the darkness, toward home.

from Ronald Reagan, *Speaking My Mind* (New York: Simon and Schuster, 1989), 410–418.

Discussion Questions

1. What two accomplishments was Reagan proudest of?
2. How did Reagan characterize the nation in 1989 as compared to when he became president?
3. Do you agree with Reagan's assessment of how the United States stood at the end of his second term? Why or why not?

PRIMARY SOURCE Civil Rights in the 1980s

When he was interviewed by Studs Terkel, Clarence Page was a 39-year-old columnist and member of the editorial board of the Chicago Tribune.

I would describe myself as a black baby boomer. I came of age in the sixties, several years after the '54 school desegregation decision. . . .

My folks were not political people. Because they were older, they tended to vote Republican. Lincoln's party that freed the slaves, you know (laughs). My father was the oldest of five brothers and the most conservative. His younger brother jumped to the Democratic Party with FDR.

Seeing the Little Rock incident on television affected me greatly. I'll never forget seeing a couple of National Guard troopers marching with bayonets on their rifles behind a couple of girls. I had not yet heard of Martin Luther King.

My mother and father were very quiet about it. I didn't find out until years later that they were very hopeful. At the same time, their feeling was, Don't make waves, don't rock the boat. Just prepare yourself, because someday the doors of opportunity would open. Be ready to step inside. They never stressed that we should try to bring that opportunity about more quickly. That came from me (laughs). . . .

The late sixties was a great time to be a black journalist. That was how I came to Chicago 18 years ago.

Something's happened in those years, hasn't it? It's become less of a civil rights struggle and more of a class struggle. It's hard for me to talk about social injustice—I'm better off than most white people are in this country. But what about the great many other blacks?

I wonder if we can any longer use civil rights tactics against economic problems. We can march for justice in Forsyth County, Georgia. We can march against apartheid in South Africa. But what do we do against the grinding problems in the black community—illiteracy, teen pregnancy, homelessness, malnutrition? We've got the poorest children of any industrialized country in the world. Civil rights marching is not going to solve it. It has to be a social justice movement in some big way.

What good does it do if you have the right to do a job, but not the education to get it? What good does it do if you have the right to go to a hotel, but

you can't afford it? You have the right to sit at a lunch counter or go to a restaurant, but . . . In some ways, we're worse off as a people today than we were twenty years ago.

There is a rage inside, an anger that certain people have tried to turn these advances around and say whatever advances black people have made have been at the expense of somebody else.

In the new racism, everybody's a victim (laughs). There are no bigots any more. A Southern leader quit the Klan and formed a new group called the National Association for the Advancement of White People. It's predicated on the notion that the whites are an oppressed class now. They borrow the rhetoric of the civil rights movement, but not its essence. Is the ex-Klansman much different from the Reagan administration that puts forth black spokesmen to oppose affirmative action because this oppresses white males?

What concerns me is that I am so alone now. There are so few blacks who have shared in this opportunity. A few of us are allowed in the door and then it's shut. . . .

It's too large for just the black middle class to solve alone. It has to be a society-wide effort. It's not just the black community. It's the Hispanic and certain parts of the white community, as well.

I think these people are worse off than twenty years ago because they are more isolated. There's less a sense of hope. I was not born rich, but as long as my family had hope, that's all that mattered. But if you don't have any hope and all you look forward to is producing more and more generations of welfare kids, you're definitely worse off. That is the big gap, the Great Divide.

from "Clarence Page," in *The Great Divide: Second Thoughts on the American Dream* by Studs Terkel (New York: Pantheon, 1988), 265–270.

Activity Options

1. Make a Venn diagram to compare Page's and Reagan's assessments of the 1980s.
2. With a partner, role-play an informal debate between Page and a member of the New Right.

PRIMARY SOURCE The First Day of Desert Storm

General H. Norman Schwarzkopf commanded the Allied forces in the Persian Gulf War. This behind-the-scenes account is from his autobiography.

The first shots of Desert Storm were to be fired at precisely 2:40 A.M. In preparation, weapons crews had labored since the previous afternoon at airfields across Saudi Arabia, Bahrain, the United Arab Emirates, and Qatar, loading warplanes from six nations with hundreds of tons of missiles, rockets, and bombs. American aircraft carriers in the gulf and the Red Sea had steamed northward, putting Iraq within range of their planes. Cruisers and the battleship *Wisconsin* had positioned scores of Tomahawk missiles in their armored box launchers for firing. Meanwhile flights of B-52s, some armed with ultrasophisticated cruise missiles originally designed to fly nuclear warheads into the Soviet Union, were closing in on Iraq from bases as distant as Barksdale, Louisiana.

A dozen high-tech Army and Air Force special-operations helicopters would start the attack. Flying in almost total darkness only thirty feet above the sand, they were to take out two key early-warning radar installations on the Saudi-Iraqi border. Behind the helicopters, eight F-15 fighter-bombers would streak into Iraqi airspace and destroy the nearest air-defense command center. That hit would, in effect, spring the gate into Iraq by opening a corridor for hundreds more airplanes headed toward targets throughout Iraq. Meanwhile, F-117 Stealth fighters were beginning bomb runs in the night sky over Baghdad.

Sitting in headquarters there was no way for us to tell at first what was going on. As each scrap of information came in, I scrawled it down on a yellow pad. . . .

Horner [Lieutenant General Chuck Horner, Air Force commander] called throughout the morning with updates as pilots and crews returned to base. By early afternoon I was able to tell Powell [General Colin Powell, Chairman of the Joint Chiefs of Staff] in Washington that we'd completed fully 850 missions. We'd clobbered many of the 240 targets on our list: Saddam's heavily defended lakeside palace in Baghdad had been annihilated; the ITT Building downtown was reportedly "glowing"; two major Scud missile sites in western Iraq had been severely damaged; the key suspected biological and nuclear

weapons bunkers had been destroyed. Meanwhile squadrons of A-10 attack jets were shooting up supply dumps along the Iraqi front lines: "They can't get reloaded fast enough," the Air Force told us. The Air Force advised that although flight crews' accuracy had been initially less than predicted—F-117s in the first wave had dropped just fifty-five percent of their bombs on target, and F-111s about seventy percent—their accuracy had been steadily improving throughout the day.

Most important, only two airplanes had gone down—an astoundingly low number, considering that we'd feared losses as high as seventy-five the first day. Horner and his planners had clearly succeeded brilliantly at undoing Iraq's high-tech defense network. By jamming and bombing its radars, they'd blinded it; by striking at its command centers, they'd paralyzed it. While pilots described how the skies over Baghdad were filled with surface-to-air missiles and antiaircraft shells, the Iraqis were firing at random with very little chance of hitting our planes. Meanwhile we shot down six Iraqi MiG and Mirage fighters. Scores more Iraqi aircraft took off from their bases, but then simply flew around avoiding our planes. . . .

At the evening briefing Burt Moore brought the news I'd been waiting all day to hear: the Army was on the move, relocating in preparation for the ground attack. On Tapline Road, the desolate two-land highway stretching west toward Jordan from the Saudi town of Hafar al-Batin near the southwestern corner of Kuwait, the heavy trucks of the XVIII Airborne Corps and VII Corps had begun moving supplies and equipment west. By the end of the first day of the war, the convoy stretched 120 miles.

from H. Norman Schwarzkopf, *It Doesn't Take a Hero* (New York: Bantam, 1992), 413–416.

Research Options

1. Research the effects of the Persian Gulf War and make a cause-and-effect diagram.
2. Research a piece of high-tech equipment that the U.S. military used during the war. Then write a brief summary to explain its use.

LITERATURE SELECTION *from* **The Bonfire of the Vanities**
by Tom Wolfe

Section 2

Set in New York City, this best-selling novel satirizes the greed and excesses of the 1980s. The novel's main character, Sherman McCoy, is the number one bond salesman at the Wall Street investment firm of Pierce & Pierce. As you read this excerpt, consider the traits and qualities that make Sherman a self-proclaimed "Master of the Universe."

At ten o'clock, Sherman, Rawlie, and five others convened in the conference room of Eugene Lopwitz's suite of offices to decide on Pierce & Pierce's strategy for the main event of the day in the bond markets, which was a U.S. Treasury auction of 10 billion bonds maturing in twenty years. It was a measure of the importance of the bond business to Pierce & Pierce that Lopwitz's offices opened right into the bond trading room.

The conference room had no conference table. It looked like the lounge in an English hotel for the Yanks where they serve tea. It was full of small antique tables and cabinets. They were so old, brittle, and highly polished, you got the feeling that if you flicked one of them hard with your middle finger, it would shatter. At the same time, a wall of plate glass shoved a view of the Hudson River and the rotting piers of New Jersey into your face.

Sherman sat in a George II armchair. Rawlie sat next to him, in an old chair with a back shaped like a shield. In other antique or antiqued chairs, with Sheraton and Chippendale side tables beside them, were the head government trader, George Connor, who was two years younger than Sherman; his deputy, Vic Scassi, who was only twenty eight; the chief market analyst, Paul Feiffer; and Arnold Parch, the executive vice president, who was Lopwitz's first lieutenant.

Everyone in the room sat in a classic chair and stared at a small brown plastic speaker on top of a cabinet. The cabinet was a 220-year old Adam bowfront, from the period when the brothers Adam liked to paint pictures and ornate borders on wood-

en furniture. On the center panel was an oval-shaped painting of a Greek maiden sitting in a dell or grotto in which lacy leaves receded fuzzily in deepening shades of green into a dusky teal sky. The thing had cost an astonishing amount of money. The plastic speaker was the size of a bedside clock radio. Everyone stared at it, waiting for the voice of Gene Lopwitz. Lopwitz was in London, where it was now 4:00 p.m. He would preside over this meeting by telephone.

An indistinct noise came out of the speaker. It might have been a voice and it might have been an airplane. Arnold Parch rose from his armchair and approached the Adam cabinet and looked at the plastic speaker and said, "Gene, can you hear me all right?"

He looked imploringly at the plastic speaker, without taking his eyes off it, as if in fact it *were* Gene Lopwitz, transformed, the way princes are transformed into frogs in fairy tales. For a moment the plastic frog said nothing. Then it spoke.

"Yeah, I can hear you Arnie. There was a lotta cheering going on." Lopwitz's voice sounded as if it were coming from out of a storm drain, but you could hear it.

"Where are you Gene?" asked Parch.

"I'm at a cricket match." Then, less clearly: "What's the name of this place again?" He was evidently with some other people. "Tottenham Park, Arnie. I'm on a kind of a terrace."

"Who's playing?" Parch smiled, as if to show the plastic frog that this wasn't a serious question.

"Don't get technical with me, Arnie. A lot of very nice young gentlemen in cable-knit sweaters

> *An indistinct noise came out of the speaker. It might have been a voice and it might have been an airplane. Arnold Parch rose from his armchair and approached the Adam cabinet and looked at the plastic speaker and said, "Gene, can you hear me all right?"*

and white flannel pants, is the best I can tell you."

Appreciative laughter broke out in the room, and Sherman felt his own lips bending into the somehow obligatory smile. Everyone was smiling and chuckling at the brown plastic speaker except for Rawlie, who had his eyes rolled up in the Oh Brother mode.

Then Rawlie leaned over toward Sherman and said, in a noisy whisper: "Look at all these idiots grinning. They think the plastic box has eyes."

This didn't strike Sherman as very funny, since he himself had been grinning. He was also afraid that Lopwitz's loyal aide, Parch, would think he was Rawlie's confederate in making sport of the maximum leader.

"Well, everybody's here, Gene," Parch said to the box, "and so I'm gonna let George fill you in on where we stand on the auction as of now."

Parch looked at George Connor and nodded and walked back to his chair, and Connor got up from his and walked over to the Adam cabinet and stared at the brown box and said: "Gene? This is George."

"Yeah, hi, George," said the frog. "Go ahead."

"Here's the thing, Gene," said Connor, standing in front of the Adam commode, unable to take his eyes off the plastic box, "it feels pretty good. The old twenties are trading at 8 percent. The traders are telling us they'll come in on the new ones at 8.05, but we think they're playing games with us. We think we're gonna get action right down to 8. So here's what I figure. We'll scale in at 8.01, 8.02, 8.03, with the balance at 8.04. I'm ready to go 60 percent of the issue."

Which, translated, meant: he was proposing to buy $6 billion of the $10 billion in bonds offered in the auction, with the expectation of a profit of two thirty-seconds of a dollar–6 1/4¢–on every one hundred dollars up. This was known as "two ticks."

Sherman couldn't resist another look at Rawlie. He had a small, unpleasant smile on his face, and his gaze seemed to pass several degrees to the right

Well, it wasn't hard to find something laughable in it, but Lopwitz was, in truth, a Master of the Universe. Lopwitz was about forty-five years old. Sherman wanted nothing less seven years down the line, when he was forty-five. To be astride the Atlantic . . . with billions at stake!

of the Adam commode, toward the Hoboken docks. Rawlie's presence was like a glass of ice water in the face. Sherman resented him all over again. He knew what was on his mind. Here was this outrageous arriviste, Lopwitz–Sherman knew Rawlie thought of him that way–trying to play the nob on the terrace of some British cricket club and at the same time conduct a meeting in New York to decide whether Pierce & Pierce was going to stake two billion, four billion or six billion on a single government bond issue three hours from now. No doubt Lopwitz had his own audience on hand at the cricket club to watch this performance, as his great words bounced off a communications satellite somewhere up in the empyrean and hit Wall Street.

Well, it wasn't hard to find something laughable in it, but Lopwitz was, in truth, a Master of the Universe. Lopwitz was about forty-five years old. Sherman wanted nothing less seven years down the line, when he was forty-five. To be astride the Atlantic . . . with billions at stake!

Research Options

1. Sherman McCoy is a top bond salesman. Find out more about the bond market. What are bonds? What are the different types of bonds? How are they bought and sold? Report your findings to your classmates.
2. A wave of financial scandals erupted in the 1980s. Research one of the people involved in these scandals, such as Ivan Boesky, Charles Keating, or Michael Milken. Then discuss with your classmates how this person compares with the fictional Sherman McCoy.

CHAPTER 25

Section 3

LITERATURE SELECTION "Salvador Late or Early"
by Sandra Cisneros

In her stories and vignettes, Sandra Cisneros creates a range of characters as varied and rich as her Chicano heritage. In this vignette, she gives a loving portrayal of a Chicano boy.

Salvador with eyes the color of caterpillar, Salvador of the crooked hair and crooked teeth, Salvador whose name the teacher cannot remember, is a boy who is no one's friend, runs along somewhere in that vague direction where homes are the color of bad weather, lives behind a raw wood doorway, shakes the sleepy brothers awake, ties their shoes, combs their hair with water, feeds them milk and corn flakes from a tin cup in the dim dark of the morning.

Salvador, late or early, sooner or later arrives with the string of younger brothers ready. Helps his mama, who is busy with the business of the baby. Tugs the arms of Cecilio, Arturito, makes them hurry, because today, like yesterday, Arturito has dropped the cigar box of crayons, has let go the hundred little fingers of red, green, yellow, blue, and nub of black sticks that tumble and spill over and beyond the asphalt puddles until the crossing-guard lady holds back the blur of traffic for Salvador to collect them again.

Salvador inside that wrinkled shirt, inside the throat that must clear itself and apologize each time it speaks, inside that forty-pound body of boy with its geography of scars, its history of hurt, limbs stuffed with feathers and rags, in what part of the eyes, in what part of the heart, in that cage of the chest where something throbs with both fists and knows only what Salvador knows, inside that body too small to contain the hundred balloons of happiness, the single guitar of grief, is a boy like any other disappearing out the door, beside the school-yard gate, where he has told his brothers they must wait. Collects the hands of Cecilio and Arturito, scuttles off dodging the many schoolyard colors, the elbows and wrists crisscrossing, the several shoes running. Grows small and smaller to the eye, dissolves into the bright horizon, flutters in the air before disappearing like a memory of kites.

from Sandra Cisneros, *Woman Hollering Creek and Other Stories* (New York: Vintage, 1991), 10–11.

Discussion Questions

1. What do you learn about Salvador from this brief description?
2. Why do you think he is "no one's friend"?

3. From what you know about his present, what do you think Salvador's future will be like?
4. Why do you think Cisneros wrote about Salvador?

CHAPTER 25

Section 2

AMERICAN LIVES Sandra Day O'Connor
The Independent Moderate

"As a judge, it is not my function to develop public policy."—Sandra Day O'Connor at her Senate confirmation hearings, 1981

Sandra Day O'Connor (b. 1930) has always held moderate to conservative political views. However, she has never followed a rigid ideology. As a politician and a judge, she has decided issues on their merit.

Sandra Day was an excellent student. She finished college and law school—which normally take seven years—in just five. She graduated third in her law school class—just two spots behind another future Supreme Court justice, William H. Rehnquist. Though she had a strong record, she could not find a California law firm willing to hire a woman. One firm did offer her a job—but only as a legal secretary. By the late 1950s, she and her husband—John O'Connor—had returned to Arizona. She was balancing her own practice with raising their children.

Sandra O'Connor entered politics in the early 1960s, working in the state Republican Party. She became an assistant attorney general for the state of Arizona and then entered the state Senate. She earned a reputation as a hard worker with a brilliant mind. In 1972 she made history, becoming the first woman ever elected majority leader of a state legislature. Though she usually agreed with conservative views, she often took a more independent course.

In 1974, O'Connor won election as a state judge. In 1981, President Ronald Reagan made history when he announced that he was nominating O'Connor to the Supreme Court. Reagan praised her "fairness, intellectual capacity, and devotion to the public good." In the Senate hearings held prior to her confirmation, O'Connor refused to say how she would rule on particular issues. The ruling would depend on the facts of the case. She did say, though, that elected legislators, not judges, make public policy. A judge's job is to interpret whether laws are constitutional, not whether they are good or bad laws. O'Connor won overwhelming support—99 Senators voted for her to become the first woman to sit on the Supreme Court.

On the Court, O'Connor has followed her moderate-to-conservative philosophy. She has often voted with conservatives on the Court. She joined them in a 1995 ruling that overturned an affirmative action law. In writing the decision, O'Connor argued that a legislature can pass laws to try to fix the effects of past discrimination. It cannot, however, pass laws that aim to shape the future makeup of a workplace or school. In another case, she joined with conservatives to strike down a Georgia plan that drew legislative districts. She objected because the plan created a district solely on the basis of race.

O'Connor does not always agree with conservative justices, however. Especially on cases that touch women's rights, she sides with the more liberal members of the Court. In one of her first opinions for the Court—*Mississippi University for Women* v. *Hogan*—O'Connor came out squarely against sex discrimination. The decision held that a nursing school could not discriminate against men. By preventing men from entering that school, she wrote, the state was actually hurting women by keeping alive the stereotyped notions of women in society. Several times she voted to uphold abortion rights.

Over time, O'Connor's vote has become increasingly important on the Court. She and two other justices have come to occupy a center position that make them swing votes. They move toward the more liberal wing for some decisions and vote with the conservatives on others. In 1993 the *American Bar Association Journal* wrote that O'Connor is "arguably the most influential woman official in the United States."

Questions

1. Who does O'Connor think should "develop public policy"? Why?
2. What do you think of the distinction that the Court made on affirmative action in the 1995 case?
3. How has O'Connor's position in the center made hers an important vote on the Court?

AMERICAN LIVES **Daniel Inouye**
Honor in Times of Crisis

"Inouye was perhaps the most patriotic person I had ever met in the sentiments that he had expressed, and I wondered how they chose this chairman—somebody who was prepared to truly be as above partisan politics as he was in this kind of affair."
—Arthur Liman, chief counsel to Senate Iran-Contra investigating committee, quoted in Sleepwalking Through History: America in the Reagan Years *(1991)*

Daniel Inouye (b. 1924) has been called on to help his country in three crises. He has served with honor and distinction each time.

Inouye was born to Japanese immigrants in Hawaii. Like other Japanese Americans, he was denied the right to join the armed forces when the United States first entered World War II. In 1943, the government finally yielded to Japanese Americans' pressure to allow them to enlist. Inouye volunteered for the army that same year. He served bravely in Europe. He won a battlefield commission as a lieutenant. Just two days before Germany surrendered, his unit was pinned down by three German machine guns. Inouye destroyed the guns despite being shot several times and having his right arm shattered by a grenade. His arm later amputated, he won several medals including the Distinguished Service Cross.

No longer able to become a surgeon as he had planned, Inouye attended law school. He entered politics and served in the last years of Hawaii's government as a territory. In 1959, Hawaii became a state, and Inouye was elected its first member of the U.S. House of Representatives. As a result, he became the first Japanese American ever to serve in Congress. Three years later, he entered the Senate.

Inouye became known as a quiet and capable senator. He backed civil rights and consumer rights legislation. After early support of the Vietnam War, he opposed further American involvement. He always voted for bills that would strengthen the nation's defenses, though. He maintained staunch support for Israel and became a leading Senate expert on foreign aid programs. Most of all, he won respect in both parties for being honest, fair, and able to work with members from both parties. It was his work on three separate committees, though, that called upon Inouye's greatest efforts.

In 1973, the Senate voted to probe the Watergate break-in and its cover-up. Inouye was named one of the Democratic members of the Senate committee investigating the matter. His fair but tough questioning earned him high regard in the Senate and with the public.

Just two years later, the nation was rocked by scandals involving the Central Intelligence Agency (CIA) and the Federal Bureau of Investigation (FBI). When the Senate formed a new committee to oversee intelligence agencies, Inouye was named to chair the committee. He worked carefully to set up reasonable controls for intelligence work. After one term in charge of the committee, he stepped down. He feared to stay on longer because he might develop "too close a relationship" with CIA officials.

A few years later, the Iran-Contra affair hit the news. Inouye was named to chair the special committee charged with investigating this affair. He set up rules that ensured that the investigation would not be marred by partisan politics. He also pushed to resolve the investigation as quickly as possible. The longer that President Reagan had the Iran-Contra issue hanging over his head, the senator worried, the worse it would be for the country. Inouye ran the investigation in a fair and serious way. When it concluded, he sharply criticized Reagan aides for their actions. They had stepped beyond the bounds of the law to set up a "shadowy" government, he said. In the United States, he reminded them, "the people still rule."

Questions

1. Why would it be bad for Inouye to have a close relationship with people in intelligence?
2. How would Inouye's fairness and spirit of cooperation be effective in a legislative body such as the Senate?
3. Why do you think Inouye was named to head the committee investigating Iran-Contra?

Name _____ Date _____

CHAPTER
26
Section 1

GUIDED READING *The 1990s and the New Millennium*

A. As you read, write notes in the appropriate boxes to answer the questions.

The 1992 Presidential Elections		
1. a. Who ran as a Republican?	2. a. Who ran as an independent?	3. a. Who ran as a Democrat?
b. Why did he fail to convince voters to support him?	b. What created an opportunity for this independent candidacy?	b. What helped him win?

The Clinton Administration's First Term	
4. What did Clinton achieve in domestic policy?	5. What did Clinton achieve in foreign policy?

The Republican Congress and the Contract with America	
6. What goals did the contract set for Republican leaders?	7. How did Clinton and the Senate undermine the contract?

B. On the back of this paper, identify **Hillary Rodham Clinton** and **Newt Gingrich** and briefly describe one success and one failure each experienced during Clinton's first term.

CHAPTER 26
Section 2

GUIDED READING *The New Global Economy*

A. As you read this section, take notes to answer questions about the U.S. role in the changing world economy.

The Domestic Economy: Good News and Bad News	
1. What was the good news?	2. What was the bad news?

The Changing Domestic Economy	
3. What trends led to explosive growth in the service sector? How were workers affected?	
4. What trends led to explosive growth in temporary work? How were workers affected?	
5. What trends led to a sharp decline in manufacturing jobs? How were workers affected?	
6. What trends led to explosive growth in the high-tech industry? How were workers affected?	

The Changing Global Economy	
7. What trends affected international trade and competition? How did those trends affect U.S. businesses and workers?	

B. On the back of this paper, explain why **Bill Gates** is a significant figure. Then tell what **GATT** stands for and what it did.

Name _____ Date _____

A. As you read about the impact of technological advances during the 1990s, note
inventions, trends, and efforts relating to each field listed below.

1. Communications
2. Health care
3. Genetic engineering
4. Entertainment
5. Education
6. Space exploration
7. Environment

B. On the back of this paper, explain the significance of the **Telecommunications
Act of 1996.**

Name _____   Date _____

GUIDED READING *The Changing Face of America*

A. As you read this section, note three facts or statistics concerning each of the
following important trends in the late 20th century.

URBAN FLIGHT The nation goes suburban.	1. 2. 3.
BABY BOOMERS The nation turns gray.	4. 5. 6.
IMMIGRATION The nation looks different.	7. 8. 9.

B. Note one challenge the United States will face in each of the following areas
during the 21st century.

1. Urban and Suburban Life	
2. Aging Population	
3. Immigration Policy	

C. On the back of this paper, define **telecommute.**

CHAPTER 26

BUILDING VOCABULARY *The United States in Today's World*

A. Matching Match the description in the second column with term in the first column. Write the appropriate letter next to the word.

_____ 1. Bill Gates

_____ 2. Telecommunications Act

_____ 3. Proposition 187

_____ 4. NAFTA

_____ 5. urban flight

_____ 6. NASDAQ

a. technology-dominated stock index

b. sought to facilitate Mexico-Canada-US trade

c. most prominent entrepreneur of the 1990s

d. leaving the cities for the suburbs

e. helped to create giant media outlets

f. cut off benefits for illegal immigrants

B. Evaluating Write *T* in the blank if the statement is true. If the statement is false, write *F* in the blank and then write the corrected statement on the line below.

_____ 1. George W. Bush won the 2000 presidential election, one of the closest in U.S. history.

_____

_____ 2. During the 1990s, many companies downsized, or added more employees in an effort to produce more products.

_____

_____ 3. Gentrification is the process of rehabilitating deteriorating urban neighborhoods and often displacing its lower income residents.

_____

_____ 4. President Clinton appointed Al Gore to lead the effort to create a sweeping health-reform bill, which ultimately met with defeat.

_____

_____ 5. High-tech businesses that did much of their business on the Internet became known as GATTs.

_____

C. Writing Write a paragraph describing the communications revolution using the following terms.

information superhighway   **Internet**   **telecommute**

CHAPTER 26

Section 4

SKILLBUILDER PRACTICE *Hypothesizing*

Hypothesizing is the process of coming up with a possible theory or cause to explain historical events. This explanation can then be tested against the historical facts to see whether it is accurate. When you read history, hypothesizing is important because it helps you understand why events occurred, what the consequences of the events might be, and what the significance of the events is. Below is an examination of the so-called "graying" of America. After reading the text, use the chart below to determine a hypothesis as well as the facts that support it. (See Skillbuilder Handbook, page R13.)

By the turn of the 21st century, America's population was increasing in age. The 2000 census revealed that Americans were older than ever before, with a median age of 35.3—two years older than a decade prior. In addition, experts predict that between 2000 and 2030, the percentage of Americans 65 and older will climb from 12.6 percent to 20 percent of the nation's population. The country's slowing birthrate, along with increased longevity and the aging of the baby boom generation are considered the primary reasons for the graying of America.

Observers fear that the growing elderly population will put a strain on Medicare, the federally funded program that helps pay medical expenses for senior citizens. The cost of the program, which exceeded $200 billion by 2000, is expected to continue rising. Concerns also abound about Social Security, which is funded primarily by taxes from the nation's younger workers, may soon run out of money. Few issues loomed as large in the 2000 presidential election as how to address the potential problems stemming from the steady growth of the nation's elderly population.

Hypothesis	Fact 1	Fact 2	Fact 3

CHAPTER
26
Section 1

RETEACHING ACTIVITY *The 1990s and the*
New Millennium

Sequencing

A. Put the events below in the correct chronological order.

_____ 1. The U.S. House impeaches President Clinton.

_____ 2. Terrorists destroy a federal office building in Oklahoma City.

_____ 3. NATO repels the Serb attack on Kosovo.

_____ 4. Bill Clinton becomes president of the United States.

_____ 5. George W. Bush is elected president of the United States.

_____ 6. The Senate acquits Clinton on his impeachment charges.

_____ 7. The North American Free Trade Agreement takes effect.

_____ 8. President Clinton is reelected.

Completion

B. Select the term or name that best completes the sentence.

welfare	Supreme Court	Congress
Kosovo	education	Chechnya
Newt Gingrich	H. Ross Perot	tax cut

1. _____ was the third-party candidate who played a significant role in the presidential
election of 1992.

2. In 1996, President Clinton signed a bill that reformed _____ by ending a 61-year
guarantee of federal aid to the poor.

3. Relations between the United States and Russia grew strained over Russia's attacks on its rebel
region of _____.

4. The _____ ended the tightly-contested presidential election of 2000 by prohibiting
any further recounts.

5. During his first months in office, President George W. Bush pushed through a _____
that amounted to $1.35 trillion over 11 years.

CHAPTER
26
Section 2

RETEACHING ACTIVITY *The New Global Economy*

Choose the best answer for each item. Write the letter of your answer in the blank.

_____ 1. The group that suffered the highest rates of unemployment during the 1990s was
    a. women.
    b. Hispanic Americans.
    c. African Americans.
    d. young people.

_____ 2. Between 1993 and 1998, union membership in the United States declined by more than
    a. 10 percent.
    b. 20 percent.
    c. 30 percent.
    d. 50 percent.

_____ 3. Bill Gates is the founder of
    a. Microsoft.
    b. Napster.
    c. America Online.
    d. NASDAQ.

_____ 4. By the end of the 20th century, the percentage of the U.S. economy devoted to world trade
was about
    a. 15 percent.
    b. 25 percent.
    c. 40 percent.
    d. 50 percent.

_____ 5. The trade agreement that lowered trade barriers and established the World Trade
Organization was
    a. GATT.
    b. NATO.
    c. NAFTA.
    d. NASDAQ.

_____ 6. The main reason that some of U.S. businesses moved their operations to other countries
during the 1990s was
    a. stronger workers.
    b. nicer climes.
    c. lower wages.
    d. greater health benefits.

Name _____ Date _____

CHAPTER
26
Section 3

RETEACHING ACTIVITY *Technology and Modern Life*

Summarizing

A. Complete the chart shown here by describing the advances made in each of the
following areas.

Area	Breakthroughs
Communications	
Science	
Medicine	

Evaluating

B. Write *T* in the blank if the statement is true. If the statement is false, write *F* in the
blank and then write the corrected statement on the line below.

_____ 1. During the 1990s, fossil fuels such as oil provided less than half of all the energy in the United
States.

_____

_____ 2. The 1990s saw the increasing use of DNA in criminal cases to prove both the guilt and inno-
cence of suspects.

_____

_____ 3. Society is unanimous in its support for research into the possibility of human cloning.

_____

CHAPTER
26
Section 4

RETEACHING ACTIVITY *The Changing Face of America*

Finding Main Ideas

The following questions deal with changes in American society at the end of the 20th century. Answer them on the space provided.

1. What factors contributed to the movement of Americans out of cities?

_____

_____

2. How did the flight of many Americans to the suburbs hurt the cities?

_____

_____

3. Why do some observers refer to the present-day as the graying of America?

_____

_____

4. What pressing issues does the nation's aging population present to American society?

_____

_____

5. How do the most recent immigrants to the United States differ from those of the earlier part of the century?

_____

_____

6. What strides did Native Americans make to improve their lives at the end of the 20th century?

_____

_____

CHAPTER

26

Section 2

GEOGRAPHY APPLICATION: MOVEMENT

The U.S. Trade in Goods

Directions: Read the paragraphs below and study the map carefully. Then answer the questions that follow.

The United States is rich in resources and industrial output. However, no nation is self-sufficient—that is, able to provide for all of its material and industrial needs. The United States therefore trades with other nations for various foods, manufactured goods, and natural resources.

The United States is a world leader in foreign trade, selling to and buying from practically every other country. U.S. companies are part of an increasingly competitive and complex struggle to find international markets for goods. Major U.S. exports include office machines, road vehicles, transport equipment, electrical machinery, general industrial machinery, and various manufactured articles. The United States, on the other hand, imports large quantities of road vehicles, electrical machinery, petroleum, clothing, office machines, and telecommunications equipment.

Ideally, a country should maintain a favorable

balance in its foreign trade—that is, export as much as or more than it imports—in order to be economically sound. From around 1900 to the early 1980s, the United States sold more to the rest of the world than it bought, creating a surplus in the balance of payments. Since then, however, the opposite has become true: the United States now imports more than it exports, and this causes a deficit in the balance of payments. In 1995, for example, the United States imported $749 billion in goods, but it exported only $576 billion.

Some countries, such as Japan, achieve a favorable balance of trade mainly through protectionism—holding down imports by means of tariffs and quotas. Therefore, in the late 1990s, the United States sought to make competition in international trade more fair by asking Japan and other countries to modify their barriers on imports.

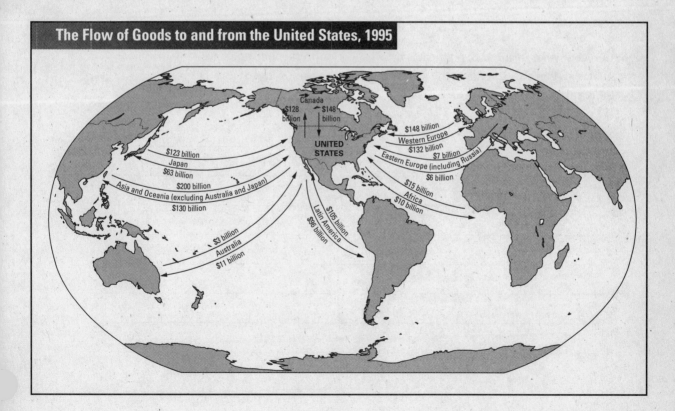

The Flow of Goods to and from the United States, 1995

Canada
$128 billion
$148 billion

UNITED STATES

$123 billion
Japan
$63 billion

$200 billion
Asia and Oceania (excluding Australia and Japan)
$130 billion

$3 billion
Australia
$11 billion

$105 billion
Latin America
$96 billion

$148 billion
Western Europe
$132 billion
$7 billion
Eastern Europe (including Russia)
$6 billion

$15 billion
Africa
$10 billion

Interpreting Text and Visuals

1. In 1995, how many dollars' worth of goods did the United States export to
   Canada? to Africa? _____

2. With which part of the world did the United States have a trade surplus? _____

   With which part was the U.S. trade most nearly in balance? _____

3. With which part of the world did the United States have a nearly 2-to-1
   trade deficit? _____

   With which area was the U.S. deficit the greatest in terms of dollars? _____

4. On the map, the Middle East is included under "Asia and Oceania." What single
   commodity—item of trade—do you think accounted for a large share of Asia and
   Oceania's $200 billion in exports to the United States?

   _____

5. In 1995, U.S. trade with Mexico amounted to $46 billion in exports and $62
   billion in imports. Would the United States still have had a trade deficit with Latin
   America without Mexico's totals?

   _____

6. In recent years, many U.S. politicians have called for protectionist policies—
   quotas and tariffs—to reduce the flow of imports into the United States. Do you
   think such protectionism is an advisable way of improving the U.S. balance of trade?
   Why or why not?

   _____

   _____

   _____

   _____

   _____

   _____

   _____

   _____

CHAPTER 26

Section 1

PRIMARY SOURCE *from* Contract with America

On September 27, 1994, more than 300 Republican candidates signed a pact called the Contract with America. The purpose of this ten-point plan, which was created by Representatives Newt Gingrich and Dick Armey and other Republicans, was to reform government, to promote economic opportunity and individual responsibility, and to maintain national security.

Within the first hundred days of the 104th Congress, we shall bring to the House Floor the following bills, each to be given full and open debate, each to be given a clear and fair vote, and each to be immediately available this day for public inspection and scrutiny.

The Fiscal Responsibility Act
A balanced budget/tax limitation amendment and a legislative line-item veto to restore fiscal responsibility to an out-of-control Congress, requiring them to live under the same budget constraints as families and businesses.

The Taking Back Our Streets Act
An anti-crime package including stronger truth in sentencing, "good faith" exclusionary rule exemptions, effective death penalty provisions, and cuts in social spending from this summer's crime bill to fund prison construction and additional law enforcement to keep people secure in their neighborhoods and kids safe in their schools.

The Personal Responsibility Act
Discourage illegitimacy and teen pregnancy by prohibiting welfare to minor mothers and denying increased AFDC for additional children while on welfare, cut spending for welfare programs, and enact a tough two-years-and-out provision with work requirements to promote individual responsibility.

The Family Reinforcement Act
Child support enforcement, tax incentives for adoption, strengthening rights of parents in their children's education, stronger child pornography laws, and an elderly dependent care tax credit to reinforce the central role of families in American society.

The American Dream Restoration Act
A $500-per-child tax credit, begin repeal of the marriage tax penalty, and creation of American Dream Savings Accounts to provide middle-class tax relief.

The National Security Restoration Act
No U.S. troops under UN command and restoration of the essential parts of our national security funding to strengthen our national defense and maintain our credibility around the world.

The Senior Citizens Fairness Act
Raise the Social Security earnings limit, which currently forces seniors out of the workforce, repeal the 1993 tax hikes on Social Security benefits, and provide tax incentives for private long-term care insurance to let older Americans keep more of what they have earned over the years.

The Job Creation and Wage Enhancement Act
Small business incentives, capital gains cut and indexation, neutral cost recovery, risk assessment/costs-benefit analysis, strengthening of the Regulatory Flexibility Act and unfunded mandate reform to create jobs and raise worker wages.

The Common Sense Legal Reforms Act
"Loser pays" laws, reasonable limits on punitive damages, and reform of product liability laws to stem the endless tide of litigation.

The Citizen Legislature Act
A first-ever vote on term limits to replace career politicians with citizen legislators.

from Ed Gillespie and Bob Schellhas, eds., *Contract with America* (New York: Random House), 7–11.

Activity Options

1. With a group of your classmates, discuss these bills and whether, in your opinion, Republicans have thus far met the objectives set forth in the Contract.
2. Work with a small group to draw up your own contract with America. Using this Republican agenda as a model, propose ten changes that you think would improve the nation.

CHAPTER 26

Section 1

PRIMARY SOURCE *from* **"A Bridge to the Future"**
by Bill Clinton

On August 29, 1996, President Clinton accepted the Democratic Party's nomination to run for a second term as president. As you read this excerpt from his acceptance speech at the Democratic National Convention, think about his vision of the future.

M y fellow Americans, this must be, this must be a campaign of ideas, not a campaign of insults. The American people deserve it.

Now, here's the main idea. I love and revere the rich and proud history of America. And I am determined to take our best traditions into the future. But with all respect, we do not need to build a bridge to the past. We need to build a bridge to the future.

And that is what I commit to you to do.

So tonight, let us resolve to build that bridge to the 21st century, to meet our challenges and protect our values.

Let us build a bridge to help our parents raise their children, to help young people and adults to get the education and training they need, to make our streets safer, to help Americans succeed at home and at work, to break the cycle of poverty and dependence, to protect our environment for generations to come, and to maintain our world leadership for peace and freedom.

Let us reserve to build that bridge.

Tonight, my fellow Americans, I ask all of our fellow citizens to join me and to join you in building that bridge to the 21st century.

Four years from now, just four years from now, think of it. We begin a new century full of enormous possibilities. We have to give the American people the tools they need to make the most of their God-given potential. We must make the basic bargain of opportunity and responsibility available to all Americans, not just a few. That is the promise of the Democratic Party, that is the promise of America.

I want to build a bridge to the 21st century in which we expand opportunity through education.

Where computers are as much a part of the classroom as blackboards. Where highly trained teachers demand peak performance from their students. Where every eight-year-old can point to a book and say I can read it myself.

By the year 2000 the single most critical thing we can do is to give every single American who wants, the chance to go to college.

We must make two years of college just as universal in four years as a high school education is today. And we can do it.

I want to build a bridge to the 21st century in which we create a strong and growing economy to preserve the legacy of opportunity for the next generation by balancing our budget in a way that protects our values and ensuring that every family will be able to own and protect the value of their most important asset, their home.

Tonight, let us proclaim to the American people we will balance the budget, and let us also proclaim we will do it in a way that preserves Medicare, Medicaid, education, the environment, the integrity of our pensions, the strength of our people.

Now, last year when the Republican Congress sent me a budget that violated those values and principles, I vetoed it, and I would do it again tomorrow.

I could never allow cuts that devastate education for our children, that pollute our environment, that end the guarantee of health care for those who are served under Medicaid, that end our duty or violate our duty to our parents through Medicare. I just couldn't do that.

As long as I'm president, it'll never happen.

And it doesn't matter, it doesn't matter if they try again, as they did before, to use the blackmail threat of a shutdown of the federal government to force these things on the American people. We didn't let it happen before. We won't let it happen again.

from *Vital Speeches of the Day*, Vol. LXII, No. 23 (September 15, 1996).

Discussion Questions

1. How does President Clinton propose to expand opportunities in the 21st century?
2. What challenges does he think must be met?
3. Why does Clinton say he vetoed the budget sent to him by the Republican Congress?
4. What American values and traditions do you think will help the United States "build a bridge to the future"?

CHAPTER

26

Section 3

PRIMARY SOURCE *from* **The Road Ahead**
by Bill Gates

Bill Gates, the chairman and chief executive officer of Microsoft Corporation, shares his vision of the future of technology and communications in The Road Ahead. *Read this excerpt to find out his views on the information superhighway.*

We are watching something historic happen, and it will affect the world seismically, rocking us the same way the discovery of the scientific method, the invention of printing, and the arrival of the Industrial Age did. If the information highway is able to increase the understanding citizens of one country have about their neighboring countries, and thereby reduce international tensions, that, in and of itself, could be sufficient to justify the cost of implementation. If it was used only by scientists, permitting them to collaborate more effectively to find cures for the still-incurable diseases, that alone would be invaluable. If the system was only for kids, so that they could pursue their interests in and out of the classroom, that by itself would transform the human condition. The information highway won't solve every problem, but it will be a positive force in many areas.

It won't roll out before us according to a preordained plan. There will be setbacks and unanticipated glitches. Some people will seize upon the setbacks to proclaim that the highway never really was more than hype. But on the highway, the early failures will just be learning experiences. The highway is going to happen.

Big changes used to take generations or centuries. This one won't happen overnight, but it will move much faster. The first manifestations of the information highway will be apparent in the United States by the millennium. Within a decade there will be widespread effects. If I had to guess which applications of the network will be embraced quickly and which will take a long time, I'd certainly get some of them wrong. Within twenty years virtually everything I've talked about in this book will be broadly available in developed countries and in businesses and schools in developing countries. The hardware will be installed. Then it will just be a matter of what people do with it—which is to say, what software applications they use.

You'll know the information highway has become part of your life when you begin to resent it if information is not available via the network.

One day you'll be hunting for the repair manual for your bicycle and you'll be annoyed that the manual is a paper document that you could misplace. You'll wish it were an interactive electronic document, with animated illustrations and a video tutorial, always available on the network.

The network will draw us together, if that's what we choose, or let us scatter ourselves into a million mediated communities. Above all, and in countless new ways, the information highway will give us choices that can put us in touch with entertainment, information, and each other.

I think Antoine de Saint-Exupéry, who wrote so eloquently about how people came to think of railroad locomotives and other forms of technology as friendly, would applaud the information highway and dismiss as backward-looking those who resist it. Fifty years ago he wrote: "Transport of the mails, transport of the human voice, transport of flickering pictures—in this century as in others our highest accomplishments still have the single aim of bringing men together. Do our dreamers hold that the invention of writing, of printing, of the sailing ship, degraded the human spirit?"

The information highway will lead to many destinations. I've enjoyed speculating about some of these. Doubtless I've made some foolish predictions, but I hope not too many. In any case, I'm excited to be on the journey.

from Bill Gates, *The Road Ahead* (New York: Viking, 1995), 273–274.

Discussion Questions

1. According to Gates, what are some of the potential benefits of the information highway?
2. Why does he think that Antoine de Saint-Exupéry, the author of *The Little Prince*, would applaud the information highway?
3. Do you agree with Gates's views on the information highway? Why or why not? Draw on your own experiences with the Internet to support your opinion.

CHAPTER 26 Section 4

PRIMARY SOURCE Road Sign

In the 1990s, the number of illegal immigrants from Mexico who crossed the United States–Mexican border at night continued to rise. Why do you think road signs like this one have been posted in California?

Copyright © Steven Rubin/The Image Works

Research Options

1. Find out how and where illegal immigrants enter the United States. Then share your findings with the class, using a map as a visual aid.

2. Research how the United States government has thus far attempted to stop the flow of illegal immigrants and then brainstorm your own ideas for solving this problem.

CHAPTER 26

Section 4

LITERATURE SELECTION Selected Poems

In the debate over immigration that has erupted at different times in U.S. history, the personal side of the issue often gets lost or ignored. For most immigrants and their descendants, the American dream doesn't come without a cost. The poems collected here present the human side of the immigrant experience in some of its varied voices.

Immigrants
by Pat Mora

wrap their babies in the American flag,
feed them mashed hot dogs and apple pie,
name them Bill and Daisy,
buy them blonde dolls that blink blue
eyes or a football and tiny cleats
before the baby can even walk,
speak to them in thick English,
       hallo, babee, hallo,
whisper in Spanish or Polish
when the babies sleep, whisper
in a dark parent bed, that dark
parent fear, "Will they like
our boy, our girl, our fine american
boy, our fine american girl?"

Latin Women Pray
by Judith Ortiz Cofer

Latin women pray
In incense sweet churches
They pray in Spanish to an Anglo God
With a Jewish heritage.
And this Great White Father
Imperturbable in his marble pedestal
Looks down upon his brown daughters
Votive candles shining like lust
In his all seeing eyes
Unmoved by their persistent prayers.

Yet year after year
Before his image they kneel
Margarita Josefina Maria and Isabel
All fervently hoping
That if not omnipotent
At least he be bilingual

Mexicans Begin Jogging
by Gary Soto

At the factory I worked
In the fleck of rubber, under the press
Of an oven yellow with flame,
Until the border patrol opened
Their vans and my boss waved for us to run.
"Over the fence, Soto," he shouted,
And I shouted that I was American.
"No time for lies," he said, and pressed
A dollar in my palm, hurrying me
Through the back door.

Since I was on his time, I ran
And became the wag to a short tail of
    Mexicans—
Ran past the amazed crowds that lined
The street and blurred like photographs, in
  rain.
I ran from that industrial road to the soft
Houses where people paled at the turn of an
    autumn sky.
What could I do but yell vivas
To baseball, milkshakes, and those sociologists
Who would clock me
As I jog into the next century
On the power of a great, silly grin.

Modern Secrets
by Shirley Geok-Lin Lim

Last night I dreamt in Chinese.
Eating Yankee shredded wheat,
I told it in English terms
To a friend who spoke
In monosyllables,
All of which I understood:
The dream shrunk
To its fiction.
I knew its end
Many years ago.
The sallow child
Eating from a rice-bowl
Hides in the cupboard
With the tea-leaves and china.

Saying Yes
by Diana Chang

"Are you Chinese?"
"Yes."

"American?"
"Yes."
"*Really* Chinese?"

"No . . . not quite."

"*Really* American?"
"Well, actually, you see . . ."

But I would rather say
yes

Not neither-nor
not maybe,
but both, and not only

The homes I've had,
the ways I am

I'd rather say it
twice,
yes

Discussion Questions

1. Which one of these poems do you like best?
   Explain your choice.
2. What did you learn about the immigrant experience from reading these poems? Point out
   specific examples in the poems.

3. Gary Soto and Diana Chang are both native-
   born Americans. How do their poems differ in
   feeling and attitude from the others? How do
   you explain the difference?

CHAPTER
26
Section 2

AMERICAN LIVES Bill Gates
Never Taking Success for Granted

"It's happening without us! People are going to write real software for this."
—Bill Gates, on seeing information about the first personal computer, 1975

Bill Gates dropped out of college—and then became the world's youngest billionaire. He has had tremendous impact on the personal computer industry. His success was achieved because he never took success for granted.

Gates (b. 1955) became interested in computers when he was only 12. At the time, computers were huge and expensive, but he and some friends learned how to write programs that could run on the machines. They began to get contracts with local companies. However, their business crashed when companies learned that Gates and his friends were high-school students.

Gates went to college, but his life changed in his sophomore year. A friend, Paul Allen, read an article about a new machine—the first personal computer. Gates was distressed. The new world of personal computers, he worried, was about to pass him by. He decided to jump in. He worked day and night to write a programming language for the new machine—even though he did not have the computer on hand and was working only from a description. When he and Allen sold the program to the computer manufacturer, Gates left college to work in the industry full time. In 1975, he and Allen formed Microsoft.

With Gates working 70-hour weeks, the company did well in its early years. The big break came in 1980. IBM—a leading computer maker—decided to build its own personal computers. Microsoft won the contract to create an operating system for the new machines. Gates bought an existing program and then worked feverishly to change and improve it. The result was MS-DOS, short for the Microsoft Disk Operating System. This program became the basic instructions for all IBM and similar computers. Each time someone bought one of these machines, he or she bought Microsoft software. Microsoft's income soared.

By the mid-1980s, Microsoft had over $100 million in sales and more than 1,000 employees. Gates decided it was time to move into new areas. One was applications software—the word processors and spreadsheets that people use to get work done. Microsoft also introduced a new operating system called Windows aimed at making it easier to use IBM-style computers.

Windows did not sell well at first, its problems were corrected in new versions and the program became widespread. Microsoft continued to grow—in sales revenue, staff, products, and influence. Soon more than 90 percent of all personal computers in the world used DOS or Windows. The company, and Gates, became subject to increasing criticism. Competitors charged that Microsoft used unfair business practices. The federal government began investigating the possibility that Microsoft actions reduced competition in the industry.

Meanwhile, Microsoft continued to grow. Many expected Gates to sit back and relax, but nothing was more unlikely. He pushed for computers to handle multimedia programs. He ordered a complete overhaul of Windows. The new version was introduced in a worldwide media blitz in 1995. Gates followed this success by launching ambitious new ventures. Microsoft began to provide access to the Internet—the global network of computers—and to put Internet links in its other programs. The company formed an alliance with a television network to provide news via cable and computer.

These steps were prompted by Gates's drive. Many computer companies had risen to the top quickly—and fallen just as fast when the industry changed. Gates has determined that Microsoft would not be one of those that fell. He feels it can stay on top by constantly meeting new trends.

Questions

1. Identify one way in which computers have changed American life.
2. Would you say that Gates played it safe in his life or took risks? Explain your answer.
3. What led some computer companies to fall from their top positions, and how does Gates intend to prevent that from happening to Microsoft?

CHAPTER 26

Section 4

AMERICAN LIVES Wilma Mankiller
Overcoming Obstacles

"Cherokee people possess an extraordinary ability to face down adversity and continue moving forward. . . . The Cherokee culture is a well-kept secret."
—*Wilma Mankiller in* Wilma Mankiller: A Chief and Her People *(1993)*

Wilma Mankiller—like her people—has an extraordinary ability to face down adversity. She gained fame when she overcame huge obstacles to became the principal chief of the Cherokee Nation of Oklahoma, the second largest Native American group in the United States.

Mankiller (b. 1945) learned of the tragic history of the Cherokees from her parents. She also learned of traditions, including self-government. In the 1950s, though, she and her family were taken off the land. New federal policy put Native Americans in cities, supposedly to enter mainstream American life. "One day I was [on a farm]," she later said, "and the next day I was trying to deal with the mysteries of television, indoor plumbing, neon lights, and elevators."

Mankiller made the adjustment. She studied sociology and became a social worker. She married and had two daughters. Then, in 1969, a group of Native Americans seized Alcatraz Island to protest federal policy toward their people. The action awakened in her a desire to join the fight for Native American rights. She felt that she could not leave her children to take part in the Alcatraz protest. She raised money, however, and became active in Native American affairs. She went to college, divorced her husband, and moved with her daughters back to Oklahoma. She built a house on her family's land and studied to complete her college degree.

With her background in social work and courses in economics, Mankiller was ready to work to improve conditions for Cherokees. Then tragedy struck. A serious auto accident almost killed her, and she needed 17 separate operations to recover. Just as she seemed to be finally recovering from the accident, Mankiller found that she had a disease causing her muscles to weaken. She had to withstand another round of difficult medical care. The setbacks gave her new dedication. "The reality of how precious life is enabled me to begin projects I couldn't have otherwise tackled," she later said.

Determined to make a difference, Mankiller went to work. She stressed that the Cherokee people could best improve their lives by helping themselves. She became head of a community development organization within the government of the Cherokee Nation. She started many new projects. One had Cherokees restore houses and build a pipeline to bring water to their homes.

In 1983 Ross Swimmer, Cherokee principal chief, invited her to run as deputy chief when he stood for reelection that year. Swimmer and Mankiller won, making her the first woman to become deputy chief. Two years later, Swimmer left for a job in the federal government, and Mankiller finished his term—becoming the first woman to head a major Native American tribe. Many Cherokees did not think a woman should be principal chief. She faced often angry opposition. However, her dedication to improving Cherokees' lives overcame prejudice. She was elected to a full term as principal chief in 1987 and reelected in 1991, resigning in 1994. In 1996 she served as a visiting scholar at Dartmouth College.

As the leader of the Cherokees, Mankiller launched many projects. She built new health clinics. One program helped Cherokee people start their own businesses. Another provided job training. Behind all the programs was Mankiller's goal: to improve the lives of her people by helping them see how they could help themselves. "We are a revitalized tribe," she wrote in her 1993 autobiography.

Questions

1. What obstacles did Mankiller overcome?
2. How did her physical problems affect her?
3. How do people benefit by working to improve their own lives instead of being told by others what to do?

Answer Key

Chapter 24, Section 1
GUIDED READING

A. Possible answers:

1. Government: Adopted the policy called New Federalism; backed a revenue-sharing bill that overhauled federal spending; used impoundment to block funding for laws that he didn't like; abolished the Office of Economic Opportunity

2. Welfare: Backed the Family Assistance Plan (FAP)

3. Vietnam: De-escalated America's involvement in Vietnam; conducted peace negotiations with Vietnam; approved illegal FBI wiretaps on left-wing, antiwar, and civil rights groups, as well as CIA and IRS investigations of those groups; oversaw FBI infiltrations of such groups; built an "enemies" list of prominent Americans; sent Spiro Agnew on a speaking tour to attack the opposition

4. Reelection: Adopted the Southern strategy to attract Southern conservative voters who were dissatisfied with desegregation and the Supreme Court; ordered HEW to delay desegregation plans; opposed the extension of the Voting Rights Act of 1965; urged Congress to halt busing

5. Court: Replaced three justices with more conservative judges

6. Stagflation: Raised taxes; cut the budget; raised interest rates; instituted wage and price controls

7. China: Adopted a policy of détente; visited China and opened up diplomatic and economic relations; signed agreements with China promising that the two nations would not try to dominate the Pacific and would cooperate in settling disputes peacefully

8. Soviet: Adopted a policy of détente; visited the USSR; signed the SALT I Treaty

B. Answers will vary widely depending upon the specifics noted.

Chapter 24, Section 2
GUIDED READING

Possible answers:

1. The plumbers' leader was an official of the Committee to Reelect the President; John Mitchell, CRP's director, had resigned as attorney general to run Nixon's campaign.

2. Judge John Sirica; to encourage the defendants who received sentences to identify others who were also involved

3. Mitchell had been Nixon's attorney general; Dean had been White House counsel.

4. Haldeman was Nixon's chief of staff; Erlichman was Nixon's chief domestic adviser.

5. a. Nixon was deeply involved in the cover-up.

   b. Nixon had taped nearly all of his presidential conversations.

6. Attorney General Richardson resigned; the deputy attorney general was fired; special prosecutor Cox was fired.

7. because only unedited tapes could provide evidence involving possible criminal activity

8. That within a week, Nixon had known of his administration's role in the burglary and had participated in the cover-up

Chapter 24, Section 3
GUIDED READING

A. Possible answers:

Ford

1. Watergate: Pardoned Nixon

2. Economy: Promoted the "Whip Inflation Now" program; tried a "tight money" policy

3. Congress: Vetoed more than 50 bills

4. Cold War: Signed the Helsinki Accords

5. Asia: Responded with massive military force to Cambodia's attack on a U.S. ship

Carter

6. Distrust: Promised never to lie to the American people

7. Energy: Advocated voluntary energy conservation; fought for passage of the National Energy Act

8. Discrimination: Appointed more African Americans and women to his administration than any previous president

9. Rights: Made human rights concerns the foundation of his foreign policy

10. Panama: Signed two treaties promising to turn over control of the canal to Panama

11. Cold War: Signed the SALT II agreement treaty

12. Middle East: Negotiated the Camp David Accords

B. Answers will vary widely depending upon the specifics noted.

Chapter 24, Section 4
GUIDED READING

A. Possible answers:

1. *Silent Spring*: Alerted Americans to the dangers of pesticide use; encouraged people to lobby Congress and the president to do something about pesticide use; helped to bring about the banning of DDT; helped Americans realize that everyday behavior affects the environment

2. Earth Day: Encouraged people to learn about environmental issues and to take action to improve the environment

3. EPA: Established regulations for, and enforcement of, the nation's environmental protection policies

4. Clean Air: Gave the government the authority to set air standards

5. Alaska: Protected millions of Alaskan acres from industrial development

6. Three Mile: Alerted people to the dangers of nuclear energy; persuaded the federal government to issue stricter safety standards and inspection procedures for nuclear power plants

B. Answers will vary widely depending upon the specifics noted.

Chapter 24
BUILDING VOCABULARY

A.

1. New Federalism

2. realpolitik

3. Saturday Night Massacre

4. Gerald Ford

5. Rachel Carson

B.

1. T

2. F—Stagflation was a combination of high inflation and high unemployment.

3. F—The Camp David Accords was a peace agreement forged between Israel and Egypt.

4. T

5. F—Under the SALT I Treaty, the United States and the Soviet Union agreed to limit the number of their intercontinental ballistic missiles and submarine-launched missiles to 1972 levels.

C. Answers will vary depending on the specifics noted.

Chapter 24, Section 4
SKILLBUILDER PRACTICE

Possible responses:

Assumption about pollution: It is a problem that has been around for a long time. Directly stated/based on evidence.

Assumption about Nixon's policies: He zigzagged between supporting business, such as the aerospace, timber, and oil industries, and creating organizations to deal strongly with the problem. Directly stated/based on evidence.

Some students may argue that the article assumes Nixon's policies zigzagged but fails to give enough examples of Nixon's support for environmental reform.

Chapter 24, Section 1
RETEACHING ACTIVITY

1. The Nixon administration increased Social Security, Medicare and Medicaid payments, and made food stamps more accessible; Nixon also tried to eliminate the Job Corps program, vetoed a bill to provide more funding for Housing and Urban Development, and impounded funds for health, housing, and education.

2. His attempt to win over Southern conservative Democrats by appealing to their unhappiness with federal desegregation policies and a liberal Supreme Court and by promising to name a Southerner to the Supreme Court

3. He hindered the civil rights movement; he ordered the federal government to delay desegregation plans for Southern school districts, he opposed the extension of the Voting Rights Act of 1965, and he attempted to stop the integration of schools through busing.

4. In an effort to slow inflation, he promoted the raising of interest rates to slow the amount of money in circulation and froze much of the nation's wages and prices; these measures eased inflation temporarily but also helped push the country into a mild recession.

5. It eased Cold War tensions, as the United States adopted a more flexible approach to dealing with Communist nations.

6. He traveled to the Communist superpowers of China and the Soviet Union, where he engaged in diplomatic negotiations.

Chapter 24, Section 2
RETEACHING ACTIVITY

A.

June 1972—burglars arrested while trying to bug the Democratic National Headquarters at the Watergate Hotel; March 1973—burglar James McCord implicates White House in Watergate burglary; June 1973—White House aide reveals that Nixon taped all his oval office conversations, prompts Congress to demand the tapes; October 1973—Saturday Night Massacre: Nixon has attorney general and his deputy fired during battle over the president's oval office tapes; July 1974—Supreme Court rules that President Nixon must turn over his oval office tapes; House committee approves three articles of impeachment against Nixon; August 1974—President Nixon resigns before full House can vote on impeachment

B.

1. He accepted bribes from Maryland engineering firms, as governor of Maryland, and during his term as vice president.

2. Obstruction of justice, abuse of power, and contempt of Congress

3. The American public and media developed a more cynical view of politicians that exists today.

Chapter 24, Section 3
RETEACHING ACTIVITY

1. c

2. a

3. c

4. d

5. a

6. c

Chapter 24, Section 4
RETEACHING ACTIVITY

A.

1. c

2. f

3. e

4. b

5. a

6. d

B.

1. F—The Alaska Native Claims Settlement Act gave Alaska's native tribes millions of acres of land for conservation and tribal use.

2. F—During the crisis at Three Mile Island, low levels of radiation began to leak from the reactor.

3. T

4. F—Americans still celebrate Earth Day each year on April 22.

5. T

Chapter 24, Section 3
GEOGRAPHY APPLICATION

Responses may vary on the inferential questions. Sample responses are given for those.

1. Oil consumption rose each year.

2. Nearly 35 quadrillion Btu

3. 1978

4. In 1973 and 1979, OPEC raised oil prices, and the resulting cost increase caused Americans to consume less oil.

5. It probably declined; just as the oil crisis of 1973 led to a two-year decrease in consumption, the 1979 price increase probably resulted in a decrease lasting for more than one year.

6. In 1973–1974, the Arab members of OPEC stopped selling oil to the United States; the United States apparently made up for the loss of Arab oil by either tapping new foreign sources or calling on nonboycotting suppliers to increase their production.

7. In the 1970s, U.S. reliance on foreign oil increased dramatically, with net imports never falling below 30 percent of U.S. consumption after 1972 and with a sharp decline occurring only after the 1979 crisis.

Chapter 24, Section 1
PRIMARY SOURCE

Newspaper Front Page

1. Informally assess students' TV broadcast re-creation.

2. Informally assess students' headlines. You may want to have students vote on their favorite headlines.

Chapter 24, Section 2
PRIMARY SOURCE

All the President's Men

Have students ask the school librarian or a librarian at a local library for help in locating *Washington Post* articles by Woodward and Bernstein. Informally assess students' summaries. As an alternative, you may want to have students research a more recent example of investigative journalism that broke a national scandal. Have them compare the impact of this news coverage with that of Woodward and Bernstein's coverage.

Chapter 24, Section 4
PRIMARY SOURCE

Love Canal

Possible responses:

1. Most people reached out to her and told her their troubles, but one woman on 97th street reacted coldly because she didn't want Gibbs to "undo what she had done" already.

2. Health problems: arthritis, miscarriages, heart attacks, migraines, kidney problems and bleeding, gastrointestinal problems, lung cancer, birth defects and crib deaths

Chapter 24, Section 4
PRIMARY SOURCE

Silent Spring

1. To find out about pesticides in use today, guide students to contact the following: a local pest control service or garden supply store, a commercial farmer, their state's Department of Environmental Conservation, the Rachel Carson Council in Maryland, or the Environmental Protection Agency in Washington, D.C. Have the class compile a list of pesticides and what insects or animals they are used to eliminate.

2. Have students contact a local health food store or an organic farmer to find out about nontoxic alternatives to pesticides.

Chapter 24, Section 3
LITERATURE SELECTION

Memories of the Ford Administration

1. First memory: watching Richard Nixon's resignation on TV with his children

2. Last memory: watching Jimmy Carter's walk down Pennsylvania Avenue to the White House after his inauguration

3. Objective research: titles of hit songs, nonfiction and fiction best-sellers, and the top TV shows

4. Some students may say Clayton thought Ford "was perfect" because he assumed office in the wake of Watergate and the resignations of Nixon and Agnew without making obvious mistakes. They may say that Clayton cites these accomplishments of the Ford administration: getting the *Mayaguez* back from the Cambodians, evacuating Americans from Vietnam, signing the Helsinki Accords, curbing inflation and slowing the recession, restoring confidence in the presidency, and pardoning Nixon. Other students may say that Clayton believed Ford was an utterly forgettable president who hardly seemed to exist; his strongest impressions of the Ford administration are of Nixon's resignation, Carter's inauguration, and his own domestic problems at home.

Chapter 24, Section 1
AMERICAN LIVES

Henry Kissinger

1. Maintain secrecy: Kissinger is right that diplomats have to keep secret the proposals that they make. Only after they have reached a tentative agreement should public debate be opened on it. Maintain openness: In a democracy, even diplomats have to work to achieve the will of the people. They should make negotiations as open as possible.

2. Agree: Unless you are using force to compel a weaker nation to do whatever you want, an agreement has to have something attractive for both parties. Disagree: Sometimes what is given up is too valuable, regardless of what is received in return.

3. Yes: The newspapers were right to publish the information. The government should not keep secrets from the people. No: The newspapers should have been stopped from publishing the information. The government has to have some secrets, especially in foreign policy, to work effectively.

Chapter 24, Section 2
AMERICAN LIVES

Barbara Jordan

1. Jordan is referring to the beginning of the Declaration of Independence and the struggle since the 1950s to provide equality of opportunity and equal justice to women and to members of minority groups.

2. Jordan was an effective lawmaker, as shown by the fact that half of the bills that she introduced were passed.

3. Jordan was saying that she thought that President Nixon was guilty of crimes that went against the Constitution.

Chapter 25, Section 1
GUIDED READING

A. Possible answers:

1. Individuals: Barry Goldwater; Ronald Reagan; William F. Buckley, Jr.; Jerry Falwell; Pat Robertson; George Bush

2. Groups/institutions: the Republican party; the New Right; the conservative coalition; intellectuals; business leaders; struggling middle-class voters; disaffected Democrats; fundamentalist Christians; the American Enterprise Institute; the Heritage Foundation; Christian televangelists; the Moral Majority

3. Issues/interests: Entitlement programs; taxes; inflation; judicial decisions; government regulation; civil rights; busing; gun control; antitrust laws; legal abortion; Equal Rights Amendment; reverse discrimination; prayer in public schools; philosophy of government; traditional moral values; divorce rates; out-of-wedlock births; individual responsibility; the size of government; government spending; national defense; pornography; the teaching of evolution in public schools; communism

B. Possible answers: Reagan's running on issues that appealed to conservatives; the Iranian hostage crisis and a weak economy under Carter; Reagan's personality and effective campaign style; Carter's weak campaign style; Reagan's skill at present-ing issues clearly and simply; Reagan's commitment to U.S. military and economic strength

C. Answers will vary widely depending upon the specifics noted.

Chapter 25, Section 2
GUIDED READING

A. Possible answers:

1. Government spending: Little change in programs benefitting the middle class; slashes in programs benefitting poorer people; tax cuts mainly for those with higher incomes; a fall in interest rates; a steep rise in the stock market; a drop in inflation and unemployment; the beginning of a recession; a steep rise in the national debt; a decline in productivity; an increase in trade imbalance; taxes raised

2. Increased military spending: The near doubling of the Defense Department budget; the revival of the MX missile and the B-1 bomber; the proposal to develop the Strategic Defensive Initiative

3. Courts: Conservative opinions on abortion rights, racial discrimination, civil rights for women and minorities, affirmative action, and the rights of arrested persons

4. EPA: Canada's pleas to reduce acid rain ignored; public land sold to developers at bargain prices; the continental shelf opened to oil and gas drilling; timber cutting encouraged in national forests; coal mining restrictions eased; Watt and other administrators forced to resign or fired following intense criticisms

B. Answers will vary widely depending upon the specifics noted.

Chapter 25, Section 3
GUIDED READING

A. Possible answers:

1. Health: The rapid spread of AIDS; the rising costs of caring for people with AIDS; legalized abortion; increasing restrictions on abortion; rising drug use; drug- and gang-related crime

2. Education: Lagging test scores; high illiteracy rates; school choice; curricu-lum innovations

3. Cities: White flight; decreasing tax revenues; high unemployment; crumbling infrastructure; poor funding for sanitation, health services, and schools; growing social problems; increasing homelessness

B. Possible answers:

1. Women: ERA not ratified; more women in public office; Geraldine Ferraro nominated Democratic vice-presidential candidate; the feminization of poverty; pay equity; new trends in divorce settlements; meager and infrequently enforced child support payments; employment benefits for families; cuts in federal day-care funding

2. African Americans: More African Americans in public office; L. Douglas Wilder elected first African-American governor; Jesse Jackson's campaign for the Democratic presidential nomination; an increasing income gap between whites and blacks; diminishing opportunities; the Supreme Court attack on affirmative action

3. Latinos: A rising Latino population in the U.S.; more Latinos in public office; the exploitation of farm laborers; the increased popularity of Latino culture; bilingual education and voting in Spanish; rising opposition to bilingual education

4. Native Americans: the decrease in federal aid; the right to open gambling casinos on reservations

5. Asian Americans: AWU founded to promote Asian culture and eliminate racist views

6. Gays and lesbians: The decriminalization of homosexual sex in seven states and 110 communities

C. Answers will vary widely depending upon the specifics noted.

Chapter 25, Section 4
GUIDED READING

Note that the distinction between Events and Trends on this chart is not absolute. Some items (e.g., the war on drugs) may legitimately be placed in either category. Possible answers:

1. Soviet Union

Individuals: Gorbachev; Yeltsin; Reagan

Events: Signing of the INF and Start II treaties; the attempted coup; the exclusion of the Communist Party from any government role; the CIS

Trends: Glasnost; perestroika; nationalism in the republics; democracy

2. Poland

Individuals: Blank

Events: A non-Communist government; a new constitution; a free-market economy

Trends: Democracy; capitalism

3. Germany

Individuals: Blank

Events: The opening of the Berlin Wall; reunification

Trend: Democracy

4. Yugoslavia

Individuals: Blank

Events: A break-up; ethnic rivalry; civil war

Trend: Ethnic rivalry

5. China

Individuals: Blank

Events: Economic reform; student marches; Tiananmen Square demonstrations

Trend: Economic liberalization

6. Nicaragua

Individuals: The Somozas; Ortega; Chamorro; Carter; Reagan

Events: Reagan aid to the Contras; secret CIA activities; the passage of the Boland Amendment; the Iran-Contra scandal

Trend: Democracy

7. Panama

Individuals: Noriega; Bush

Events: The overthrow, arrest, and conviction of Noriega for drug trafficking

Trends: "Yankee imperialism"; the war on drugs

8. Iran

Individuals: Reagan; North; Bush; Lawrence E. Walsh

Events: The taking of hostages;

Reagan's secret arms sales; the Iran-Contra scandal; congressional investigation; indictments; Bush pardons

Trends: Blank

9. Iraq

Individuals: Hussein; Schwarzkopf; Bush

Events: The invasion of Kuwait; Operation Desert Storm

Trends: Blank

Chapter 25
BUILDING VOCABULARY

A.

1. b

2. a

3. c

4. c

5. a

B.

1. e	5. f
2. d	6. b
3. g	7. c
4. h	8. a

C. Answers will vary depending on the specifics noted.

Chapter 25, Section 1
SKILLBUILDER PRACTICE

1. President Ronald Reagan; a speech before the American public.

2. Ayatollah Ruhollah Khomeni

3. Reagan misled the American public when he told them that the United States was not engaged in an arms-for-hostages deal with Iran.

Chapter 25, Section 1
RETEACHING ACTIVITY

A.

New Right: definition—right-ring grass-root group; views—supported school prayer and opposed abortion, Equal Rights Amendment, busing, and affirmative action; Conservative Coalition: definition—alliance of business leaders, middle-class voters, dis-

affected Democrats, and fundamental Christians; views—promoted conservative policies; Moral Majority: definition—evangelical and fundamental Christians; views—condemned liberal attitudes and argued for a restoration of traditional moral values

B.

1. actor, spokesman for General Electric, governor of California

2. The weak economy and the prolonged Iranian hostage crisis

3. He was comfortable on the public stage and adept at simplifying issues and offering concise and clear-cut answers.

Chapter 25, Section 2
RETEACHING ACTIVITY

1. budget cuts, tax cuts, increased defense spending

2. The cuts slashed funding to many of the programs on which the poor relied, such as urban mass transit, food stamps, welfare benefits, job training, Medicaid, school lunches, and student loans.

3. Tax cuts along with a decline in interest rates and inflation bolstered the public's confidence in the economy and prompted them to go on a spending spree. In addition, the stock market soared, unemployment declined, and the gross national product began to grow.

4. They ended liberal control over the Court that had begun under Franklin Roosevelt.

5. The administration cut the budget of the EPA, and ignored pleas to reduce acid rain; the secretary of the interior, James Watt, sold millions of acres to public land to private developers, opened land to gas and oil drilling, encouraged timber cutting in national forests, and eased restrictions on coal mining.

6. Business people, many of whom wanted to deregulate the economy; Southerners, who welcomed limits on federal power; Westerners, who resented federal controls on mining and grazing; Reagan Democrats, who thought the Democratic Party had drifted too far to the left

Chapter 25, Section 3
RETEACHING ACTIVITY

1. c

2. b

3. a

4. a

5. b

6. d

Chapter 25, Section 4
RETEACHING ACTIVITY

A.

1. Berlin Wall

2. Iran-Contra

3. Kuwait

4. Commonwealth of Independent States

5. Panama

B.

1. F—As part of his *perestroika* plan, Mikhail Gorbachev called for less government control of the economy.

2. T

3. F—The Boland Amendment banned military aid to Nicaragua for two years.

4. F—the United States organized an international coalition to help it repel the Iraqis.

5. T

Chapter 25, Section 3
GEOGRAPHY APPLICATION

Responses may vary on the inferential questions. Sample responses are given for those.

1. In 1990, about 19.4 percent of all Latinos in the United States lived in Texas.

2. Nine; Latinos made up about 8.5 percent of the population of the middle Atlantic region in 1990.

3. There were 1,437,720 Latinos living in the east north central region of the United States in 1990.

4. 42; New York

5. East south central

6. California and Texas

7. Third; fifth; although the mountain region contained fewer Latinos than either the middle Atlantic or the south Atlantic region, its total population was far smaller than the total populations of those regions, so Latinos made up a greater percentage of its population.

8. Many Mexican Americans have settled in the Southwest because it is the part of the nation nearest Mexico. Also, Mexico has historical ties to that part of the United States, since much of it was formerly Mexican territory. Many Cuban immigrants have settled in Florida because it is close to Cuba. Latinos are also concentrated in industrial states—such as New York, New Jersey, and Illinois—since many jobs are available in those states.

Chapter 25, Section 4
OUTLINE MAP

1. Mediterranean Sea, Suez Canal, Red Sea, Gulf of Aden, Arabian Sea, Strait of Hormuz, and Persian Gulf

2. United Arab Emirates, Qatar, Bahrain, Saudi Arabia, Kuwait, Iraq, and Iran

3. Saudi Arabia

4. Egypt

5. Cyprus and Bahrain

6. Jordan and Iraq

7. Europe, Asia, and Africa; Turkey (mostly in southwestern Asia and with a small section in southeastern Europe) and Egypt (mostly in Africa and with a small section—the Sinai Peninsula—in southwestern Asia)

Chapter 25, Section 2
PRIMARY SOURCE

Political Cartoon

1. Firemen are trying to rescue someone with a net.

2. The "safety net" will not catch anything because it has no bottom.

3. Students may say that Reagan's eco-

nomic strategy of cutting social programs leaves only the illusion of a safety net for the poor.

Chapter 25, Section 2
PRIMARY SOURCE

Ronald Reagan's Farewell Address

1. Reagan was proudest of economic recovery and the recovery of morale in America.

2. He said it was more prosperous, more secure, and happier.

3. Some students may agree that the United States was strong and prosperous and was still a magnet for those seeking freedom. On the other hand, students may point out that the nation faced a host of social and economic problems such as the spread of AIDS, rising drug abuse, and a soaring national debt.

Chapter 25, Section 3
PRIMARY SOURCE

Civil Rights in the 1980s

1. Informally assess students' Venn diagrams.

2. Informally assess students' role-playing.

Chapter 25, Section 4
PRIMARY SOURCE

The First Day of Desert Storm

1. Informally assess students' diagrams. Effects may include the following: Kuwait's liberation, a cost of $61.1 billion to the United States, the deaths of 85,000 Iraqis, President Bush's high approval rating, environmental problems caused by burning oil wells, physical problems of veterans caused by exposure to chemicals.

2. Informally assess students' summaries.

Chapter 25, Section 2
LITERATURE SELECTION

The Bonfire of the Vanities

1. Through their research, students will find that bonds are written promises to repay a fixed amount of money on a specified date and to make payments of interest at regular intervals in the interim. They may also find that there are corporate bonds issued by corporations; government bonds such as savings bonds, Treasury bills, and Treasury bonds; and municipal bonds issued by nonprofit organizations such as public hospitals, cities, and school boards.

2. Informally assess students' discussions.

Chapter 25, Section 3
LITERATURE SELECTION

"Salvador Late or Early"

Possible responses:

1. Salvador is one of those anonymous, poor Chicano kids who must take care of his younger siblings. He is ignored by his teacher and his classmates and perhaps even his family. His self-esteem is so low that he apologizes every time he speaks.

2. Salvador is no one's friend because he is always busy taking care of his younger siblings. He has no time to stop in the schoolyard to play with the other children.

3. His future will probably be filled with hard work and care-giving. He may have a loving family, which will be some consolation.

4. Cisneros probably wants her readers to be aware of children like Salvador—those selfless, self-sacrificing Chicano kids ignored by others.

Chapter 25, Section 2
AMERICAN LIVES

Sandra Day O'Connor

1. O'Connor thinks that legislatures should make policy by passing laws because they are elected by the people and so are more responsive to the people.

2. Agree with the distinction: It makes sense to try to repair injuries caused by discrimination in the past but not to set aside preferences based on racial or other characteristics. Disagree with distinction: Affirmative action will help Americans create a diverse workplace and society, which is a valuable goal.

3. O'Connor has become important because she represents a swing vote on the Court, moving to the conservatives on some decisions and to the more liberal members on others.

Chapter 25, Section 4
AMERICAN LIVES

Daniel Inouye

1. Inouye was probably concerned that if he became too close to the people whose actions he was supposed to monitor, it would be more difficult for him to monitor them effectively.

2. In a legislature, it is necessary to work with people of many different views–in the case of the Senate, with people from both parties. By being fair and cooperative, Inouye could win the trust of members of the other party.

3. Inouye was named to chair the Iran-Contra investigating committee because of his experience with Senate investigations, because he was familiar with intelligence activities, and because his reputation for fairness meant that the investigation would be less likely to be criticized.

Chapter 25, Section 1
GUIDED READING

A. Possible answers:

1. Republican
   a. Bush
   b. Failed because he raised taxes after promising not to; lacked an economic strategy for dealing with the recession

2. Independent
   a. Perot
   b. Weak economy; voter discontent

3. Democrat
   a. Clinton

b. his promise to move away from traditional Democratic policies and his focus and fostering greater economic progress

4. Domestic: a diverse cabinet; deficit reduction; welfare reform; a proposed health care bill; low unemployment

5. Foreign: The passage of NAFTA; helping to preserve a fragile peace in the former Yugoslavia; increased trade with China at the expense of human rights

6. Goals: Congressional term limits; a balanced budget amendment; tax cuts; tougher crime laws; welfare reform

7. Undermined: opposed Republican budgets that slowed entitlements and federal aid programs

B. Answers will vary widely depending upon the specifics noted.

Chapter 26, Section 2
GUIDED READING

A. Possible answers:

1. Good news: creation of ten million new jobs; low unemployment

2. Bad news: Flat or declining family incomes; widening income gap between rich and poor

3. Service: The changeover from a manufacturing to a service economy; the jobs created were mainly temporary or part-time, low-paying, with few benefits.

4. Temporary: Corporate downsizing; full-time staff replaced with temps who earned less, received fewer benefits, and had little job security

5. Manufacturing: growth of the service sector as well as automation; workers laid off or forced to work for far less money; fewer workers represented by unions

6. High-tech: Computers; an increased demand for workers with advanced training and specialized technical skills; higher paying jobs among "knowledge workers"

7. International: The adoption of free-trade agreements increased international trade and competition; some growth in U.S. manufacturing jobs;

businesses pressured to cut costs, leading to job insecurity; job flight to cheaper labor markets overseas

B. Answers will vary widely depending upon the specifics noted.

Chapter 26, Section 3
GUIDED READING

A. Possible answers:

1. Communications: The information superhighway; the Internet; e-mail; the World Wide Web; the personal computer; the cellular phone; the fax machine; the "smart" office; the "bodycam"; the removal of barriers that had prevented communications companies from conducting more than one type of communications business; the V-chip

2. Health care: More accurate diagnoses, less painful treatments, and more effective medications and treatments; magnetic resonance imaging; the use of virtual reality to diagnose health problems

3. Genetic engineering: The increased availability of genetically altered food products; public concern over genetically altered foods; FDA approval of genetically altered foods

4. Entertainment: Video games; virtual reality; the CD-ROM; the Internet

5. Education: The CD-ROM; the Internet; greater classroom access to computer networks; an increased classroom use of long-distance video and audio transmissions

6. Space exploration: The Hubble Space Telescope used to gather more information about the formation of stars and galaxies; NASA's *Pathfinder* and *Soujourner* transmit live images from Mars; building of International Space Station

7. Environment: Greater efforts made to develop environmentally friendly vehicles, such as electric cars, solar cars, and cars that run on ethanol or methanol gas; increased recycling of aluminum, paper, glass, etc.; increased efforts to develop technology for cleaning up large oil spills; increased efforts to replace fossil fuel with alternate energy sources, such as nuclear, solar, and wind energy

B. Answers will vary widely depending upon the specifics noted.

Chapter 26, Section 4
GUIDED READING

A. Among the many possible answers:

Urban flight

1. By the early 1990s, about 43 percent of the Latino population and more than half of the Asian-American population lived in the suburbs.

2. The 2000 census indicated that affordable suburban housing was booming in many states.

3. In 1990, the 31 most impoverished communities were in cities.

Baby boomers

4. By 2000, the median age of Americans was 35, two years older than a decade prior.

5. By 2030, 1 out of 5 Americans is expected to be over age 65.

6. By 2005, spending on programs benefiting the elderly is expected to consume 39 percent of the federal budget.

Immigration

7. In the 1990s, about 45 percent of immigrants came from the Western Hemisphere and 30 percent came from Asia.

8. By the early 1990s, there were an estimated 3.2 million illegal immigrants.

9. The proportion of non-Latino whites to minorities is expected to continue to shrink.

B. Possible answers:

1. Urban and suburban: A decline in the economic base of cities and an increase in suburban wealth

2. Aging: The possibility that the Social Security system will not be able to support retired senior citizens

3. Immigration: Dealing with illegal immigration

C. Answers will vary widely depending upon the specifics noted.

Chapter 26
BUILDING VOCABULARY

A.

1. c

2. e

3. f

4. b

5. d

6. a

B.

1. T

2. F—During the 1990s, many companies downsized, or trimmed payrolls to streamline operations and increase profits.

3. T

4. F—President Clinton appointed Hillary Rodham Clinton to lead the effort to create a sweeping health-reform bill, which ultimately met with defeat.

5. F—High-tech businesses that did much of their business on the Internet became known as dotcoms.

C. Answers will vary depending on the specifics noted.

Chapter 26, Section 4
SKILLBUILDER PRACTICE

Hypothesis: The increase of America's elderly population will present the nation with a number of significant challenges.

Fact 1: The cost of funding Medicare is rising.

Fact 2: Social Security funds may run out.

Fact 3: Care for the elderly has become a key political issue.

Chapter 26, Section 1
RETEACHING ACTIVITY

A.

1. 5	5. 8
2. 3	6. 6
3. 7	7. 2
4. 1	8. 4

B.

1. H. Ross Perot

2. welfare

3. Chechnya

4. Supreme Court

5. tax cut

Chapter 26, Section 2
RETEACHING ACTIVITY

1. d

2. d

3. a

4. b

5. c

6. b

Chapter 26, Section 3
RETEACHING ACTIVITY

A.

Communications—explosive growth of the Internet, emergence of the information superhighway, growth of telecommuting; Science—virtual reality training for pilots and doctors, surgeons perform long-distance surgery, space modules reach Mars and beam back live pictures, researchers map the genes of the human body, growth of genetic engineering; Medicine—improvement in battling cancer and AIDS, use of MRIs to more closely examine the body

B

1. F—During the 1990s, fossil fuels such as oil provided 85 percent of all the energy in the United States.

2. T

3. F—A number of groups, including politicians, ethicists, and religious leaders, believe that human cloning is dangerous and immoral.

Chapter 26, Section 4
RETEACHING ACTIVITY

1. overcrowding, increasing crime rates, decaying housing

2. The flight of so many people and jobs shrunk the cities' tax base and

hindered their ability to provide services.

3. The 2000 census revealed that the median age of Americans had grown and that the number of Americans 85 and older grew at a faster rate than any other segment of the population.

4. The need to keep Medicare and Social Security well-funded in order to meet the growing demand for care to the elderly and disabled

5. Most of the nation's earlier immigrants came from Europe, while a majority of the new immigrants have come from Latin America and Asia.

6. Dozens of tribes attained greater economic independence by establishing gaming resorts. In addition, a number of tribes have won greater recognition of their tribal ancestry and land rights through the courts.

Chapter 26, Section 2
GEOGRAPHY APPLICATION

Responses may vary on the inferential questions. Sample responses are given for those.

1. $128 billion; $10 billion

2. Australia; Eastern Europe

3. Japan; Asia and Oceania

4. petroleum (oil)

5. No, it would have had a trade surplus of $7 billion.

6. Yes: the only way the United States can achieve a favorable balance with such protectionist countries as Japan is to adopt protectionist policies of its own. No: protectionism will simply result in retaliation from other countries, making it more difficult for the United States to export its goods.

Chapter 26, Section 1
PRIMARY SOURCES

Contract with America

1. Before students begin to discuss the Contract with America, suggest that they refer to pages 850–852 for information about bills passed by the Republican Congress. Then infor-

mally assess students' discussion.

2. Responses will vary but should include concrete suggestions for making the nation safer, more just, and more prosperous.

Chapter 26, Section 1
PRIMARY SOURCE

"A Bridge to the Future"

1. Clinton plans to expand opportunities through education and training.

2. Challenges: reducing crime, breaking the cycle of poverty and dependence, balancing the budget

3. He vetoed it because the budget violated Democratic values and principles; according to Clinton, the proposed cuts threatened Medicare, Medicaid, education, the environment, and pensions.

4. Students may say that such traditions and values as freedom, democracy, a spirit of entrepreneurship, creativity, ingenuity, hard work, and so forth will help the United States build a bridge to the 21st century.

Chapter 26, Section 3
PRIMARY SOURCE

The Road Ahead

1. Benefits: increase understanding, reduce international tensions, allow scientists to collaborate more effectively on finding cures, help students pursue their interests

2. Saint-Exupéry would applaud because the goal of the information highway is to bring people together.

3. Some students may agree, citing their own personal experiences of finding valuable information and connecting with others by means of the Internet. Others may disagree because, despite the benefits in improving and expanding communication, they fear that the information highway could eliminate the traditional concept of community, increase isolation, and result in a loss of privacy. They may cite their experiences with surfing on the Internet to back up their opinions.

Chapter 26, Section 4
PRIMARY SOURCE

Road Sign

1. Through their research, students will find that many illegal aliens migrate north to cross the 1,952-mile-long border between Mexico and California, Arizona, New Mexico, and Texas. They may also find that paid guides known as coyotes help them cross the border without getting caught.

2. Through research, students will find that the Border Patrol, which was created in 1924, conducts searches to capture illegal immigrants and patrols the border to stop illegal aliens from entering the country. Also, the 1986 Immigration Reform and Control Act outlawed the hiring of illegal aliens and strengthened controls to prevent illegal entry into the United States. You may want to have students share their brainstorming ideas with the class.

Chapter 26, Section 4
LITERATURE SELECTION

Selected Poems

Possible responses:

1. Opinions should be supported by explanations.

2. Anxiety about having your children accepted by mainstream America in "Immigrants"; fears and difficulties associated with the English language in "Latin Women Pray"; negative stereotyping and being accepted for who you are in "Mexicans Begin Jogging" and "Saying Yes."

3. Soto's and Chang's poems are more humorous and lighthearted than the others. The speakers in both poems seem perfectly comfortable with their ethnic heritage and American identities; it is others who are confused.

Chapter 26, Section 2
AMERICAN LIVES

Bill Gates

1. Education is different because research can be done more quickly using computer search tools and because simulation games make learning more lively and interesting.

2. Gates took risks. For instance, he quit college to write programs full time even though he did not have a job.

3. When leading computer companies did not keep up with changes in technology, they lost their leadership position. Gates watches trends carefully to ensure that this does not happen to Microsoft.

Chapter 26, Section 4
AMERICAN LIVES

Wilma Mankiller

1. She had to overcome the injuries from the auto accident, her illness, and the prejudice of male members of the Cherokee Nation.

2. Mankiller's physical problems convinced her to work to make a difference.

3. When people work to improve their own lives, they learn valuable skills and gain pride in their accomplishments, which can help them do more.

CURRICULUM